School-Boy Reminiscences, a Poem

Schoolboy Rreminiscences

BIBLIOBAZAAR

SCHOOL-BOY REMINISCENCES.

A Poem.

BY AN UNDERGRADUATE.

CAMBRIDGE: J. AND J. J. DEIGHTON.

1844

TO

THE REV. J. CARTMELL, M.A.

FELLOW AND TUTOR

OF

CHRIST'S COLLEGE, CAMBRIDGE,

This Volume

IS

WITH PERMISSION DEDICATED

BY

HIS EVER GRATEFUL AND OBEDIENT SERVANT,

THE AUTHOR.

May 24, 1844.

PREFACE.

THIS poem, which I lay before the Public, is intended to be a slight description of those hours that the boy spends in the halls of Science; and I have introduced any recollections that may have particularly struck me at that period. At first it was my intention to dwell entirely upon the Classic Poets that are most usually read in schools; but having been a traveller, my mind could not rest in so limited a sphere.

A friend, to whom I read it, observed that there was a part in the second Canto of Marmion, from which I might be accused of stealing some ideas. Speaking of a convent, I have used the title Hilda, a title I remembered that I had seen elsewhere, but had forgotten the precise book, not having read Marmion since my boyhood, the circumstances of which particular part had quite escaped my recollection. I merely have added this to escape the imputation of borrowing from others.

If this book is written in a melancholy strain, it was caused by a heavy pressure of mournful circumstances. To the land of the South my thoughts most frequently wandered, where some part of my juvenile days was spent, and, I may add, some of my happiest hours. Australia has been hurled to the very lowest depths of misfortune since my departure (which is now some years), and many a dear friend, whom I once beheld in the zenith of prosperity, has been hastened by reason of its desperate condition to a most untimely end: if this be no excuse for a melancholy strain pervading my poetry, I desire to offer no further apology. As I have written nothing *particularly* relative to Australia in my poem, I send this small token on the southern breezes to her:—

Australia! when a boy I left thy shore,
Thy parting smile to me beamed beautiful:
There was a wild song in the farewell roar
Of thy rude billows; and the young sea-gull
Had music in its shriek; which came more full
Upon my heart, because it was the last.
'Twas a soul-piercing sound! which oft did rule
My aching bosom in the adverse blast;
'Twas that soul-piercing sound, which never shall be past!

On that bright morn our vessel left thy port—
Madly I could have burst the swelling sails,
And, stung with overwhelming, frenzied thought,
Have sent their pieces to the whistling gales!
'Tis well indeed intention often fails;
For how could I behold thee prostrate now?
'Tis well indeed my mournful vision hails
Old Albion's laughing hills; though here will flow
Too oft Grief's blood, as if thorns pierced my beating brow!

Lo! the Pacific's sweetly azured breast,
Tinged with gold dolphins' loving summer's sun,
Heaves bitterly; and mourns that she, so blest
In her fair childhood, should be now undone!
Undone, alas! and who, yes, who but One,
Can e'er allay her pangs, or heal her breach?
Ah! ships that hail this isle now so alone,
See the "thick darkness" round her glittering beach—
May God soon sheath his flashing sword, or patience teach!

SCHOOL-BOY REMINISCENCES.

INTRODUCTION TO CANTO I.

To write, yet be original, this day,
Is something half impossible: but still
My feelings swell, my passions own no sway,
As mounting Helicon's subliming hill!
Exulting here, feel subject to no will;
Nature lies stretch'd before me—there I roam;
Though man's invectives round may echo shrill;
Creation's boundless range my heart's wide home;
Free to its oceans, mountains, valleys, I now come.

With these I shall converse, as man with man,
And hold my dialogues with calms and storms;
The mighty globe is no inferior span,
Where wanderers, long ere this, have traced its forms:
Heaven's opening coliseum, which ever warms
The breast with thrilling joy, doth high expand;
Its towering dome inspires, yet half alarms;
Arch'd in a moment by supernal hand,
The Almighty's fearful footstool, by his wisdom plann'd.

Ocean of feeling! sweet, thy depths to dive,
Thy gilded beach of sand my best delight,
Thy rocks around make spirit, soul, alive,
Thy trembling bed my crystal cradle bright,
Where spangling planets soothe away the night.
On thy long-famed expanse I love to ride,
And gazing round, oft cheer'd me with the sight;
The pearl-like richness of thy heaving tide,
Where oft Imagination sail'd in glory's pride.

'Tis sweet to indulge on fair Cithæron's height,
'Tis sweet to see the yellow Xanthus flow,
'Tis sweet to fancy climes of buoying light,
Where mild ambrosial summers ever glow:
And sweet to view Parnassus white with snow.
'Tis sweet to mark young Beauty ripening forth,
Like Chinese flowers, which endless blossoms show,
Nursled in painted jars, where tempests' wrath
Can never dim their streaks, nor vile Destruction's moth.

How sweet to dream of Childhood's days again,
By woodland lakes, and forests' shady haunts!
To drown, as then, the thoughts of woe and pain,
All self-implanted care and fancied wants:
Oh, while recalling them, the bosom pants,
As exiles feel when longing to return
To their own native land! where Feeling plants
The dearest stores in Nature's social urn,
Where day's expanding sunlight seems to brightest burn.

'Tis sweet to view the deep sea, like a child
With calm blue eyes and with unspotted mind;
When its empurpled face gleams undefiled,
And not the gentlest breeze a bower can find:
When the world-shaker sleeps by peace refined;
And Silence reigns there with cerulean crown,
Filletting all her coral curls, that wind
Down to her lily bosom: when no frown
Is looking from the jewell'd gates of Neptune down.

'Tis sweet, when clouds along the welkin rush,
To see the sailor climb the giddy masts,
Furl the sheets 'mid the universal crush,
As the skiff battles with the unheeding blasts:
Oh, how exulting, as each billow casts
Ideas of god-like splendour in the soul!
Ah! yet it frights man when such wonder lasts.
Roll on, ye inspiring elements, yet roll,
Where Biscay's royal bosom heaves you to each pole!

Some deem him fanatic who loves to tread
The towering mountains, man to leave afar;
Who tries the thunderbolt's dark page to read,
And flinches not in elemental war:
My soul, spurn such! oh, turn Heaven's door ajar,
For there are mysteries which make passion swell:
Great joy! to seek proud heights in Fancy's car;
From here though many an avalanche low fell,
Yet yon superior Powers calm whisper, "All is well."

Even such my boyhood loved: to roam steep hills,
Where cities looked mere specks, and empires mounds;
Even this my elated mind full often thrills,
Though more advancing age my brow surrounds.
When the tall Pyrenees' ennobling bounds
Rise in colossal pride, their peaks unfurled,
There perched ambitious in the Elysian grounds,
To boast o'er Italy's and Gaul's far world,
Standing upon their cloud-robed tops 'mid lightnings hurled!

Here busy nations never feel the charm;
Where beautifully sloping hills arise,
And fill the gazer with a glad alarm,
All girt round by emparadising skies:
Here lulled in Philomela's touching cries,
Start quite transported, and heaven's raptures steal;
Where the soul gazes with its endless eyes
On radiant pleasures which can well regale:
Hope standing on their lofty brow can never fail.

With daffodilies some would strew the main,
And plant blue violets on its smooth sands
Of teeming gold, to wave in brilliant reign;
And make young Muses cull with lily hands
Their perfumed blossoms; and they would form lands
To grow them bowers of pink geranium,
Mingled with ivy's sheen, and give them wands
To make all loveliest things spontaneous come;
Thus their imagination builds its sunny home.

Away with this! let me reflect on Time:
How its wings droop with countries' destinies;
The nameless shade they spread o'er many a clime,
To see depicted life's real miseries.
On swift wings Pleasure comes—on these she flies
Far, far away; the simple word of truth,
Though seeming sullen, makes ungarbed to rise
Things in their stern reality; forsooth,
This tells the impartial news alike to age or youth.

CANTO I.

I.

Who sound the lyre in ages like to these?
Who dare to string its death-snapped chords again?
What! leave it toneless? even the sighing breeze
Would tune its shattered chords, invoke its strain!
The lonely Muse kneels in her honour'd fane,
While suppliant eyes pierce her once mortal race,
Who now review her from immortal plain:
A full tear trembles on her saintly face—
Shall no one dare come forth that tear afar to chace?

II.

Horrid offenders surely are those men,
Who say that mind is wanting to the Muse;
That, though her lines sound nobly now and then,
Through narrow gate great Knowledge does diffuse
Its stores to him who her attention woos.
"Behold the frenzied dreamer!" thus they cant;
"He builds towers that in air importance lose,
" Which base and other requisites so want.
He shews them toys, by felling them to others plant."

III.

There are, who, when alone in midnight cell,
Affirm hobgoblins, and forms lacking names,
Flash full before them, breaking that strange spell
Which chains the dead in catacombs' pale frames:
Sometimes, they say, they see Hell's towering flames;
Sometimes the New Jerusalem in flights
Of wild delirium! Such are maniacs' dreams.
Not so with dreams which yield the Muse delights;
She sits on Fame's high peak; composed and calm
there writes.

IV.

The throne of Fame how hard is it to gain,
A pardon grant if youth be over rash!
For who can tell how grand must be that strain
Which falls on Fame's ear, yet does not abash?
Since too such heartless critics are to lash
The flinching mind, how fearful 'tis to write;
For critics' words wound far more than the crash
Of tempests o'er our roof at black midnight!
May the bard's years plead some for lines with error
dight.

V.

Yet, "still, small voice" of Wisdom, speak to me;
I love thee better than the trump of Fame!
Let drums, and fifes, and bugles' breath agree
To inform earth's millions of the conqueror's aim.
Let Buonapartes but time's vain laurels claim,
Let them astound the world for life's short hour;
Shew me how turn they dust from whence they came,
How dark the Gothic domes above them tower;
Oh, shew my heart how soon dissolves all mortal power!

VI.

And though from fount of earthly fame thou drawest,
Still feed at heaven's great breasts my unweaned soul;
For there eternal nutriment thou hast.
Yonder in endless page thy name enrol.
For this world's glory has a bounded goal;
And though not despicable meant to be,
Yet Providence ne'er destined this man's whole;
There o'er his eyes smiles immortality!
This ever keep in view. Stop! what is this I see?

1.

From the mount that views Corinth I looked upon Greece,
As its landscape was sleeping in beautiful peace;
From the Acro-Corinthus, transcendent as yet,
I glanced to the distance, and saw her sun set!

2.

From the mount that sees Corinth I wept on that land,
Which appealed to my soul, oh, how painfully grand!
Not a murmur arose—not the slightest of sound,
As her hill-altars lay in their ruins around.

3.

On the pillow of exquisite silence she slumbered,
Her conquests were over, her days were all numbered;
But she seemed, like some Peri from climes of the blest,
In the bosom of Earth only taking her rest.

4.

Yet her time-revered shores were resplendent and bright,
Yet her long-sacred ocean was glowing in light!
And I thought of bright galleys once sailing it o'er,
Of the heroes and chiefs that would sail it no more.

5.

And a Sophocles, Æschylus, once could adorn
That first clime of their hopes, now bereft and forlorn;
An Alcæus and Sappho, with thousands now gone,
Who have long left her childless—to weep all alone.

6.

O thou land of the great! did Destruction think fit
That thy Corinth to Bondage' vile yoke should submit;
That patriots should see Athens from summits of bliss,
Hurled with Græcia's state grandeur down Fate's dark abyss?

7.

Even still, Chæronæa, Remembrance repines,
As she muses how Macedon's thick-phalanxed lines
Spoke a world to the Greeks in the trumpet's dread strain,
When thy day, Independence, seemed fast on the wane!

8.

Years have glided, yet oft I recall that sad eve,
When a Greece, I beheld, but beheld it to grieve;
And my soul, though afar from time's seasons of ill,
If allowed, in the grave shall remember it still!

VII.

Have ye seen the land where Helle's hallowed ocean
Tells of the days of history, and of old;
Where, as the billows roll in troublous motion,
Weeps Græcia's sun in fading fire of gold?
Abydos lies in woe's abyss deep rolled!
Oh! 'tis not now the clime of matchless love!
Upon that widowed coast no more unfold
Its riches to the eye. Ah! as we rove
Over those ancient borders, Death frowns from above.

VIII.

All ye who hail with rapture foreign shores,
Look at Abydos in your glorious way,
Just cast one glance on her decaying stores
Of beauty, which once had sublimer day:
Exult not, smile not! for the tempest's spray
On you some fatal hour may dash the same;
But think how once, in majesty's array,
She cheered the seaman, as he saw her flame
With force, with energy, which had a brighter name!

IX.

O thou, whom better days, whom happier hours,
Ought to have waited, now I sing of thee;
The clime where Love's unmatched, undying powers
Left time to live in immortality!
Where perished sad the once divine and free.
Past are those unforgotten times; yet breathe
Their dreams in Sestos' sadness, as we see
The last of such sweet hours in woe beneath,
Gliding in grief far off upon thy storm, O Death.

X.

And suns, and moons, still gild Abydos' coast—
But are they beautiful as those of yore, [boast,
In which young Freedom's sons could make their
And wished such seasons smiled for evermore?
Oh, from yon sacred height, how I adore
Thy once so grand domain, illustrious Greece!
I feel the darkest passions swell and soar;
My bosom owns, even basest senses cease
To banish Sympathy, and uncouth Nature please.

XI.

Great, immemorial Bards! your songs no more
Shall soothe the lands where Venus courted Fame,
When virgin Fortune rose upon that shore,
Which was, and is, unequalled yet the same!
Where loved Apollo reigned, and made his claim
On you, the authors of his favourite verse,
Which still for ever lives through years of shame;
While ye are fallen 'neath that woeful curse
Which Adam's sin brought down, which must soon all
immerse.

XII.

I am now musing on a faded time,
On days for ever fled; and Ruin's throne
Stands on the downfal of that Asian clime;
Her heroes on Destruction's wings have flown:
The heartless Moslem even heaves the groan,
Reading of Hero's, and Leander's fate;
Looks he on Helle's sea, which seems alone
To weep, while thus the seamen to him state,
The legend of the rock where loveliest Hero sate.

XIII.

"The Hellespont frown'd dark, the winds were high,
Heaven's giant brow was red with eve's past heat;
And clouds and thunders galloped through the sky,
In an alarming crash to loudly meet!
The waves, like mountains, shook the boundless sheet
Of waters, and the voice of Cupid shrieked
'Tween sky and ocean, and night's coming feet
Most madly trembled; while Creation creaked
Upon its polar hinges—Hell its vengeance reeked!

XIV.

The concave ball of heaven, in horror spread,
Blazed with sheet-lightning; one fierce mass of blood
Which sullied all the sky with boding red,
Cynthia stared, like a maniac, o'er the flood
Of thunders, lightnings, blasts, in awful mood
Commingled! Thus the wan moon sometimes seems
Amid eclipsing tempests, scowling rude;
Her fair face dabbled o'er with ghastliest gleams,
Frowning unnatural to earth with gore-stain'd beams.

XV.

Midway 'tween Sestos' and Abydos' seas
A human figure tumbled in the main;
Firm as the bark which ne'er the billows flees,
Clustering around it in colossal train:
A distant torch was fluttering o'er the plain
Of ocean, brandished from enormous height:
The struggling being thus answered it again,
By waving hurriedly to where the light
Was held by virgin hands. Oh, who describe this night!

XVI.

Around that castled cliff the midnight's veil
Lowered in ire, Leander not yet here;
While Hero's features, turning deadly pale,
Sunk into frenzy, mocked each rising fear:
Down her unsullied cheeks no glittering tear
Made its still pilgrimage; but maddened thought,
Dark as those clouds upon the eternal sphere,
Shaded her broken feelings, which now sought
Repose in ocean's caves—there lie a thing of nought.

XVII.

Expiring glory now illumed her face:
Before, by sorrow urged, she dared to leap
Down the low, low abyss; and one might trace
A beatific halo gently creep
Round her dark eyes, ere closed in deathly sleep:
Like to a dying twilight did it shed
Its faint flood there, where hardest hearts could weep;
The last of woman's splendour sought to wed
That immemorial maid, ere resting with the dead.

XVIII.

The shores of Greece then glimmered in her mind,
She sighed adieu to its immortal isles;
Where Love a native birth-place first could find.
She seemed just as a sinking rainbow smiles
Through fading storms; possessing richer wiles,
As the ethereal hues in arms of death
Sad fainting, e'en the tempest's gaze beguiles;
Thus Hero looked ere leaving all beneath,
From whose clear brow had lastly fled Hope's ambient
wreath.

XIX.

In one dark stream adown her snowy neck,
Her hair flowed on the banners of the wind!
She thought not of herself. O hateful wreck
Of light, love, glory, beauty, thus combined!
Her piercing eyes even Fancy's sight could blind,
Fair in their madness, exquisitely wild!
She looked some demi-goddess sent to bind
The rough sea in strong fetters, make it mild.
Now, ere she dashed her down, she gazed towards heaven, and smiled.

XX.

From the tall height she sprang! the flaming brand
O'er the dim scene electric glances cast;
Clenched still in firmness by her upraised hand,
Unconquered flames amid the howling blast!
Like a young Cybele of ages past,
She tinged the waves as sinking in the deep,
And shed those charms, too enviable to last,
Upon that sea where she desired to sleep,
Where sirens, it is said, the fruits of ocean reap.

XXI.

They sank within the deep, but rose no more!
Alas! that is an unforgotten night;
And still the legend haunts old Sestos' shore,
Of which illustrious bards have loved to write.
Broad Heaven was rolled in ire, a monstrous sight,
With swelling clouds, and Anger's haughtiest scowl;
The tempest-claps roared with unequalled might,
About the lounging rocks did idly prowl,
And ocean's azure diadem became a cowl.

XXII.

Farewell, sad lovers! still the moonlight's tear
Shall oft bedew your Helle's ocean-cheek;
As listening starlight makes a pause to hear,
Once more upon that sea, the piercing shriek:
When Sestos' maid, but tinged with Venus' streak,
Leaped like the thunder into Neptune's wave;
With that form yet incomparably meek,
She rudely plunged beneath the boisterous grave,
That yawned asunder, dashed her to some pearly cave.

XXIII.

The Rock of death still frowns on Sestos' coast;
On Helle's deep are nightly shrieks of woe;
There tramples on the main a pallid ghost,
When cloud-embattled gales in vengeance blow:
A spirit waves a torch-light o'er that brow,
Its features wild, yet grander than the storm;
The fearful fisher sees it spring below,
While Love, with magic fire, appears to warm
Its thrilling aspect, ere the waves close o'er that form!"

XXIV.

Even in youth's earliest dawn I had like tale
Breathed in my ear—and magical it seemed;
At night upon my ear arose the wail,
When the last pride of Sestos no more beamed!
Oft of Leander, Hero, have there gleamed
Thoughts 'mid the charming visions of that youth;
Their unexampled love, my spirit deemed
As some fictitious tale that has no truth,
Save when my fancy longed to realize them both.

XXV.

May we not feel indeed, events like these
Could animate old age—much more those souls
Who, but as Genius' younglings, felt her breeze;
Could give the theme which monarchs'breasts unfolds?
The war of Troy, whose glory to the poles
Shines forth; and History's great and numerous deeds
Did this. And many a fable which enrols
Truth in its painted volume, now oft leads,
And formerly oft led, to where Redemption feeds.

XXVI.

Her bands select on Helicon's blest mount,
Where a bright country the glad eye salutes;
From whose green bosom Hippocrene's clear fount
The Muses' fading energy recruits;
Oft on its glassy wave have lovers' lutes
Made the sweet melody in measures float,
And pierced the heartless nerves of earth-prone brutes.
Here sounded forth of old the harping note
Of those whose chords with tones of poesy were fraught.

XXVII.

Not Homer, foremost in the ambrosial ranks
Of celebrated poets, struck the lyre;
Though halls of Science pay devoted thanks
To him, and would his ashes now inspire.
The Muse first nursed Amphion's kindling fire,
Linus', Musæus', Thamyris', Orpheus' strains;
These, History says, lived ere the Homeric choir
Enraptured Scio's soil, and soothed the fanes,
Which now, on hills laid waste, look sad towards Græcia's plains.

XXVIII.

Oh, unforgotten times, eternal hours,
Ye haunts of memory, realms of bye-gone bliss!
Ah! when thy muse, O Scio, sought the powers
Of Fancy's divination, thought he this?
Could he imagine Ruin's deep abyss
Would swallow such fair beauty in its hell?
Alas! the footsteps of the famed we miss!
The traveller looks, tears quit their crystal cell;
Each breeze moans in his ear like some far-echoing knell.

XXIX.

Yet daily suns o'er-gild this Scian isle,
Yet pleasing reminiscences abound;
The Galiongi hails with brightening smile
From the tossed deck its fair shores glistening round.
Here in the dark blue ocean has he found
'Mid the Æolian blast a port of joy.
When Nature has her starlight halo wound
O'er striking ruins glimmering 'neath the sky;
Glance on its form the scenery thrills you, far and nigh.

XXX.

Far o'er the deep sea answering to the gaze,
Where buoying recollections fire the soul,
Beams this enamouring clime of other days;
And seamen land, escaping many a shoal:
Oh! as their barks upon the billows roll,
The evening sea-birds skim the azure plain,
As welcoming them to the Scian goal.
Inspired with love, linked by affection's chain,
The sunset sheds such charms, they seem at home again.

XXXI.

Undying records, which the heart sublime,
Meet you on every peak ye take your stand;
Filled is Idea with the Homeric rhyme,
It elevates, and does a power command!
Magnificently noble, truly grand,
The remnants of the past their summits rear;
Proudly exalted, clasping hand in hand,
Fame, Glory, Honour, crown this care-worn sphere,
Though centuries are past, in youth they yet appear.

XXXII.

And has the rod of vengeance to thee come,
O Isle of Scio? Sibyls answer, "Yes"!
That rod has also struck my happy home,
Where once were halycon days of pleasantness;
Where from a child I did bright Fortune bless,
Because she cooped me 'neath her golden wing,
Even as the bird her youngling. Then distress,
Mid, oh how joyful scenes! I e'en would fling
From my thoughts, nor knew I a disappointment's sting.

XXXIII.

But hear the words that Anger would respire,
Driving submission far. "Though I transgress,
Yet woe shall never quench the unconquered fire
Burning within Pride's breast: no God I address.
Inured to grief, at last I grief caress,
And if a cannon-ball struck on my frame,
The hardy crocodile not own it less:
The Avenger's scourge shall not my spirit tame!"
Ah! this the enthusiast's wrath; this only ends in shame.

XXXIV.

Wights oft there are, who prowl in cells of grief,
Imagining it sentimental seems;
And if they write, their pen is labouring chief
With gloom to stigmatize their anxious dreams;
Dread pictures scowl through their poetic gleams.
Not so with him whose is this artless lay;
He who guides Nature's changing wheels and schemes,
Has deemed it fit to hedge about his way,
And now to cloud the skies of his once-cloudless day.

XXXV.

'Tis for the best. Then hail, avenging scourge!
That like the midnight ghost, would scare life's dreams;
It has an end, when heaven intends to purge
Some foul recess, where, as yet, no ray beams!
Well, be it so; my soul the hint esteems.
Although the viper wound with poisonous dart,
And though the venom, mingling with life's streams,
Staunch the vain current in this mortal heart,
It shall make my immortal act a nobler part!

XXXVI.

The ruined city a just awe commands;
Behold its columns lying desolate,
Its weed-grown streets enlivened by no bands,
And prostrate sunken its triumphal gate!
Type too predictive of man's short estate;
To-day in bliss, to-morrow doomed for dust,
Fortune's smiles darkening into frowns of Fate:
Then rots upon his shadowy throne the crust
Of garnished hollow tinsel, all that he could trust.

XXXVII.

Then Grief, that vile arch-spectre 'mid our gloom,
Whom on the battlements of storms we see
Environed by black clouds, hurls down the boom
Of anger on our heads, and strips our tree
Of hope. Ah! musing thus, I own to be
Our great tormentors the remembered dead;
We sigh on their still graves—'tis agony!
And haggard-visaged Vengeance stoops to read
From off the marble page, how swiftly such have fled.

XXXVIII.

Survivor of the gallant crew I feel,
Though in their shattered bark I sailed not
With them through life, through all its woe and weal:
Yet, as if had been fixed with them my lot,
They wear the mien I never yet forgot.
Yes, they were sucked down by the ruffian surge,
Lashed from life's shaggy cliffs, like weeds to rot;
But though their mortal frame the big waves merge,
Their immortality e'er lives our thoughts to urge.

XXXIX.

Developing so ably heroes' deeds,
We almost hear the din of battle roar,
The clashing shields and spears, as Fancy reads
Expressive lines in the Homeric lore.
Peruse the Odyssey; it seems to explore
The byeways of the human character.
Observe his scenes: the much-resounding shore
Seems to me reading round each verse to stir,
As if transplanted to the spot I really were.

XL.

O Inspiration! now bestow thy tongue;
Enable me to celebrate the praise
Of Græcia's Scian muse, who loved, and sung
Upon, the enlightened lyre of ancient days!
Near forest lakes the antlered stag obeys
His hermit-master, when he tunes his harp;
His fine neck arches, and the enkindled rays
Burn in his eyes. Let his example warp
Base feelings from their course. Oh! all my errors carp.

XLI.

For shall I have such taste as to forego
The quiet of the student's midnight lamp,
To quaff the cup of Wickedness full low
To the vile dregs; to strive all thoughts to damp;
And Conscience' mighty energy to cramp
Amid the lustre of the heating wine?
No! let research' desire in triumph stamp
On airy shapes of Vice which seem divine;
This brings its fruits, the other causes us to pine.

XLII.

Homer's great lines imagination coy
To ruminate on Ida, and remark
The scenes which would a Sybarite annoy,
Dilapidated Ilium, frowning dark!
Desolate now the abodes, where the fierce spark
Of red Contention made Troy's walls to blaze,
Like stormy Morning's crimson. Hark, yet hark!
For Desolation issues forth to raze
A track, a remnant even of that city's praise.

XLIII.

Parent of inextinguishable deeds!
Nurser of bravest offspring! born to drink
From youth the blood of War! Remembrance feeds
The insatiate appetite on acts that sink
Into Fame's rocky page; there like stars wink.
Ida! how thy tall peaks bear me along
Amid the rush of fancy; and I think
Of hours now gulphed in death; while shadows throng
Of the past round my brain, inspiring Sorrow's song.

1.

As I viewed Xanthus' streams from old Ida's famed hill,
Oh, how could I have swum in effusions of joy!
But, struck with past memory, my heart 'gan to fill,
And I thought upon Ida, but wept upon Troy!

2.

For the fire of its death flashed again full anew,
And it blazed on their waves as they rolled to the shore;
While the war-smoke in volumes curled thick to my view,
And 'mid huge flames of grandeur did Ilium deplore!

3.

Look afar—what black vapours bewilder the sky!
List! the shrieks of the Trojans once more rend the air:
Oh, now hear the o'erwhelming, the desolate cry!
See! their Hector has fallen 'mid yells of despair.

4.

But the spell of a strong fascination is over,
And the reverie broken, Troy looks as it is;
The demons of Death o'er her last remnants hover
How they howl on the rapid decay of her bliss!

5.

Did not Ida once smile on the seasons that rolled
In the pride of their beauty for many a long mile?
Oh! that beauty still pilgrims of Nature behold,
Ida also remarks it, but no more can smile.

6.

As the streams of the Xanthus wound sadly along,
They appeared to flash back the destruction of Troy,
Where through war-renowned halls no more flowed
battle's song,
And where never again shall be banquets of joy!

XLIV.

Renownèd Hesiod! thy Bœotia grieves,
But grieves in vain. Enchanters ne'er recall
The dead of centuries. Thy glory weaves
Such path thro' Greece that makes us mourn thy fall.
The Atropos has long outspread the pall:
She never turns. Thy monument shall brave
The rush of uncouth hurricanes. The ball
Of heaven shall oft demolish many a grave;
Yes! empires too; but thine the strength of Power shall
save.

XLV.

Piled on the clouds of Fame, what can it screen?
Allow your cogitations their repose
On Helicon at noon-day's cool serene.
The wreck of glorious Ascra braves the woes,
Which long since might have been the fatal close
Of other lands' career. The herds, the flocks,
Feed on Bœotian pasturage; Nature bows,
Arrayed in evening's grandeur! Such oft shocks
The halting stranger; for this scene the sad truth mocks.

XLVI.

Lesbos, oh, Lesbos! though life's web is broken,
Redemption's halo lingers o'er thy scenes;
Glory yet leaves upon thy hills her token,
Her pledge 'tween every vacuum intervenes!
Abode of better days! the student gleans
An information from thy relics strewed
In masses on the earth: even thus he weans
Himself from emptiness; he seems imbued
With that same fire lost by thee, but in him renewed.

XLVII.

She emerged, proud as the Oceanus of old,
Enriched with sons and daughters; on her head
An Iris gleamed; the azure waves turned gold
Where'er her feet of loveliness would tread:
Purple streams were most copiously shed
Around her bosom; of celestial white
Glistened her raiment; dimples too did wed
Her smiling cheeks angelically bright—
Alas! how soon a sunset dimmed that healthy light.

XLVIII.

A stormy sunset thy last sunset was;
Electric mists rushed from Hell's solitude,
And none explained, nor could explain, the cause.
Oh, wrathful darkness on thy brow did brood,
Despair's black visage scowled upon thee rude!
Yet, Lesbos, hast thou still a power for me,
With nameless fascination art thou hued,
With unclothed aspect shining gloriously—
Even in thy naked form a deathless charm I see!

LXIX.

Thy days, fair Sappho, long have run their course,
Yet was their distant goal eternity:
Have they not ended but to approach the source
Where star-isles twinkle in the blooming sky?
There are the climes that gold can never buy!
But Virtue gratis to their height shall come,
Expatiating there shall never die;
There in the plains of Freedom shall she roam,
There shall she tabernacle in her endless home.

L.

Let Envy with Imagination shape
The ideal of loveliness, we seldom find,
In its perfection; let us Beauty ape
Through the wide loop-holes of the picturing mind.
From Fancy's mould let Sappho rise refined,
With young protecting Hymens by her side;
Let Cytheræa's wreath her temples bind,
That the sun might by such be well defied;
Expression paints her eyes, while borne through rapture's tide;

LI.

Like some black storm, when sunlight glimpses thro'
The rolling surface of the splendid heaven;
Which though o'erveiling its interior hue,
Magnificence to every shade is given!
Even such a storm as oftentimes is driven
Around cloud-poising Teneriffe: yet find
A match for woman's eyes! I oft have striven,
But all earth's princeliest splendour seemed behind;
Suns, moons, stars, rainbows, whate'er flame the giddy kind!

LII.

Hair as profoundly dark as well can be,
Floating luxurious down a neck of snow;
A neck like polished marble, that we see,
That marble taught by sculptor's art to glow.
Leucadia-wandering pilgrims even still show
The rock from which she sprang with frenzied leap;
And when the planetary waters flow,
At glorious midnight, round this starlight steep,
The mermaids, riding on the billows, stay to weep.

LIII.

Sappho, oh, Sappho! when thy bosom swelled
With poesy's wild and melodious strains,
Alcæus was thy willing captive held,
Alcæus felt the softness of Love's chains!
Amid the Lesbian night a planet reigns,
Whose silvery voice doth thy past songs rehearse,
And its harmonious cadence never wanes,
But through the stilly hour its rhythmic verse
Loves to lull all to rest, the shepherd's cot to nurse.

LIV.

Books there exist of rich accounts, which say
That lunar rainbows smile on the blue deep,
And stride the sky's empyrean, broidered gay,
That there they, like young Aphroditæ, sleep:
The moon has condescended them to steep
In starry streams by nothing e'er defiled;
And, looking on them, travellers oft weep,
So overcome they are by streaks so mild,
Painting the clouds, and air, and ocean's barren wild.

LV.

Tinged by pale Cynthia's rays, and blending with
The aerial showers, great beldam Nature sees
A dreamy form soon injured by Time's scythe,
Dissolving in the bosom of the breeze.
Such was the Sappho of an ancient Greece!
Too delicately moulded long to last,
Too beautiful. Near her the savage knees
Might by devotion's bands be fettered fast;
A lovely spirit of a vision so soon past.

LVI.

Oh! how Alcæus melted 'neath her gaze;
How he rejoiced in Passion's swimming trance;
As sunlike did the overpowering rays
Of imagery from her features glance!
These and these are the hours which life entrance,
These make us all past agonies forget,
These, these are compensation's pleasing grants,
These hours so inexpressible, so sweet!
And yet 'neath time's horizon how soon do they set!

LVII.

I hear a voice behind me gently singing,
And whispering to me of those brighter ages;
Interpreting Fame's volume, and thus bringing,
In vivid colours, all the immortal sages.
O voice of History! which the child engages,
Dear are thy lessons, musical thy words:
What admirable wonders gild thy pages;
Thy endless theme an endless search affords,
Where graven are th' exploits of this world's mighty lords!

LVIII.

And thou, most-famed Arion! whose renown
Has reached our ages, been triumphant through
The horrid changes that have come and flown
On whirlwind-pinions—thou unknown by few!
Weeping on Mitylene we renew
A fresh acquaintance with those that have died.
And never have we sailed o'er waves more blue,
Than those that land our bark on Lesbos' side,
Which never to the outcast entrance has denied.

LIX.

A tribe of dolphins, so the proverb tells,
Conveyed thee safely from a treacherous host
Of murderous seamen; and o'er shining swells
Of Amphitrite, took thee their treasured boast,
Unto the cliffs of Tænarus' far coast.
Thy lyre entranced them as they skimmed the tide
Of dimpling Neptune; in its richness lost,
The chords of joyance gave them wings to glide,
And on this mystic beach they laid their bosom's pride.

LX.

Divinely matted in its foliage green,
The Lesbian scenery greets the wandering stranger;
Heaven smiling on it in a calm serene.
Emparadising clime of sons which were!
Oh! if, perchance, the boughs make rustling stir,
And the leaves fall on earth with startling sound;
'Tis but that, falling, they may not incur
The fault of failing, though it yield a wound,
To wake the wanderer's soul to those beneath the ground.

LXI.

Sleep they beneath the turf, but not unheeded;
Yet are their ashes dear as Iran's gold:
Fair as her native isle, has Sappho pleaded
With blunted heart that deigns not to behold
In awe Titanian structures 'fore it rolled;
Which ne'er recoiled at Babylonia's waste.
Yet o'er her tomb its passions could unfold
Themselves, and love's expression be upraised;
While mourning, to sierras lone, that heart might haste.

LXII.

There weep the tears it never wept before,
There feel what it may never feel again;
Though it should travel far from shore to shore,
Meet empires' ruins stretched on hill and plain.
With genius' death is linked the shaft of pain;
And if that creature too were beautiful,
From minstrel-bosom pours a gloomier strain;
The inhospitable heart seems overfull,
Where now the dew of pity for the first bears rule.

LXIII.

Ye isles upon the ocean-blue of Greece!
That, like to storm-tossed gems, are glittering yet;
The emblem, that your Glory ne'er shall cease,
Is seen amid Fame's suns that never set!
What hallowing sight indeed the eyes have met,
Watching in frenzy the still-lingering ray
Of your once brighter smile we ne'er forget;
While, in seas gilted round, the sad display
Of dying evening typified your better day!

LXIV.

For here the blending hues of memory pass
In colours very deep, in swathes of fire;
Like to the dazzling sparks in shattered glass,
Which make us dizzy, as sunbeams inspire
The gorgeous fragments. Yet, ah! yet inquire,
"Who can the broken pieces once more mould;
Who, as the wild sighs from his breast respire,
Could with invention's tools dare task so bold,
That we might in its pristine beauty Greece behold?"

LXV.

'Tis vain. Still, Heaven, regard the suppliant's prayer!
Now let my pencil, dipped in golden ink,
Attest to noble Greece the mad despair
That would to her fair shores my ardour link!
O Love, transporting Love! let hermits think
That selfish haunts are blest without thy light:
I drink, I quaff, I quaff, and yet will drink
Again, again, from out thy waters bright;
And walk the storm upon the Iris of thy might!

LXVI.

O'erwhelming in thy sweetness and thy style,
Fosterer of elegance, and lyric verse,
Anacreon! idle hours I could beguile
Reading thy poems, there my soul immerse.
It seems upon the present race a curse
To weigh thy style, which us of glory strips:
Degenerated, yes! becoming worse;
We shall in heaven soon witness boding stripes,
The muse clothed in an everlasting dark eclipse!

LXVII.

O love-heavenizing muse! whose dulcet lyre,
When to its full melodious pitches strung,
Conveyed a wild and passionate desire,
But left a Cadmus' vast exploits unsung.
Oh! how ambitions have my ears oft rung
With airy echoes, lingering o'er thy odes;
The heart's strings, my mind roaming them among,
Vibrated back; as when I hear in woods
The chirp of linnets twittering in sweet green abodes.

LXVIII.

Then, as triumphant as the eagle's cry,
When from the forest mountain he takes wing
To dart along the broad and lonely sky,
Those echoes heightened! and how did they bring
Delightful tones that made my nerves to ring;
Thoughts and ideas too mighty to express,
Transporting sounds to which we all would cling!
They came upon each feeling with such stress,
That never after such could I love this world less.

LXIX.

Who thinks of Myrtis' and Corinna's powers,
Nor hails with interest the Pindaric muse?
Who thinks of Thebæ's once meridian hours
That burnish'd Time's proud annals, nor such woos?
For 'twas no common power, which could infuse
Olympian heat within the very core
Of their raised understandings; to arouse
With rhythmic measures, and enlivening lore,
The wide arena crowded as was ne'er before.

LXX.

And now, as in my humble path advancing,
Are lights of immortality about;
Beams of peculiar loveliness are glancing,
Like those in woman's orbs that take their route:
A glorious route! Beams fairer than the fruit
Of painting's ever-shadowy device:
Myrtis and young Corinna cast a doubt,
So deeply black and glittering their eyes,
Whether they are not fairy Houris of the skies.

LXXI.

The bees buzzed round his lips, so authors say;
From whence, as he lay sleeping on the grass,
The honey juice exuded; and the day
Of his great greatness after came to pass:
Mythology states such the intrinsic cause.
How afterwards he shone in Fancy's bowers;
And in the music of each vocal clause,
Shewed Poetry's omnipotence—her powers—
That on high seat above the world the proud Muse towers!

LXXII.

How sweet, rich, overpowering, were the tones
Of his fair teacher Myrtis! such her strains,
That they moved mighty monarchs on their thrones,
And held them captives in Euterpe's chains:
That high-pitched melody which gives the reins,
Whereby we madly worship to excess,
And makes the blood rush wildly through the veins.
As the young actress' breast doth so caress
The eye of youth, it shews off harmony none the less.

LXXIII.

Oh! passion, feeling, energy, and love,
High-mindedness, and greatness, sought to raise
The soul of Pindar to the realms above,
To indulge in splendour of immortal blaze.
Peruse his matchless odes, it well repays;
The grand, free rhythm that lifts the heart to heaven!
Which, while ye read, invokes unto the gaze
The beauty of the spot that he has given,
Such beauty to describe not in vain has he striven.

LXXIV.

See how celestial lies in landscapes spread
Elsusis' scenery! Twining foliage
Can Nature's calm adorer ever wed;
Exquisite ramble for the musing sage.
Sweet spot! thou didst my stripling thoughts engage;
Thou wert the sainted shore of feeling's tide,
Where Glory did reveal the foolish rage
Of thy base enemies, who would oft bid
Us to reject thy relics that for e'er abide.

LXXV.

Long-hallowed haunt! which many a deathless act
Has made to studious minds the holiest spot:
Looking on thee if energy e'er lacked
Its pathos, 'twas that memory forgot.
Here is it Meditation mourns the lot
Of Science' bright career, so frailly short;
Of those whose works, howe'er their bones may rot,
Shall ne'er expire, shall never turn to nought,
But by Research, years rolling on, be better sought.

LXXVI.

The palm of Victory in books, and wars;
The undaunted laurel charmingly displaying
Æschylus' brow, the prey of wounds and scars;
For his was patriotism life outweighing!
Poet and warrior; at the same time swaying
Mars' falchion, and the sceptre of the Muse:
And young Melpomene to the Thunderer praying,
Mailed him in battle-plains, that every bruise
Not injured him, but changed to Honour's brilliant hues.

LXXVII.

O Arethusa! whose bewitching name,
Like sea-breeze' dulcet notes, for ever gave
To Syracuse an everlasting fame;
Whose fountains' trickling, all its outskirts lave.
Of old, of happy times, thy lucid wave
Sacredly pure tells every stander by;
Revealing, as it would one's pity crave,
The unsullied hours of thy virginity;
Thy skill in archery with many an one could vie.

LXXVIII.

We read that in thy present stranger clime,
An Æschylus did close his great career;
That he who dignified the Attic rhyme,
Made, by his exit, most renowned thy sphere.
Wisdom stands bulwark to her sons for e'er;
Did he shrink 'neath that final hour? Why, no!
Intellect takes up arms against despair;
It makes the shoulder bear its load of woe,
It calms the dying mind, as life's scenes dimly glow.

LXXIX.

Enough to call, in ages like to these,
Curse equal to Kehama's on our heads,
To think the Muse with modern lines agrees,
That round our page her lucent taper sheds
Its beams. Alas! 'tis not for us she dreads
To make a Dagon of antiquity;
Still Æschylus, such like, she ever weds,
And spurns our compositions from her eye—
There, burnt in Hades, let them in their ashes lie!

LXXX.

An eminence there is consigned to fate;
One temple crowns its brow, by History sought;
A noble temple of an ancient date,
Whose columns are fast crumbling into nought:
It is Colonos—oh, how sweetly fraught
With many a dream of Tragedy's loved child!
Here had his powerful intellect the thought
Of mightiest grandeur, when it was beguiled
By themes so beautiful, although so madly wild!

LXXXI.

And he who strays there, views the bright blue sea,
Then looks on sad Colonos' shattered site:
It is a gem of immortality;
Though now it but possesses ruined might.
Have ye sate there amid the starry night,
And thought upon its memorable brow?
Then well ye understand there dwells a light
Unquenchable in Beauty's eye when low
Even in the sad grave, which makes the tomb to glow.

LXXXII.

O Muse-nursed child of immemorial worth,
Great Sophocles! on yonder solemn peak
Thou didst to those effusions give a birth,
Of which the very world feels proud to speak.
Round that famed steep a halo's dimpling streak
Tells of the glorious days of thy renown;
There are the haunts the cultured mind would seek,
And muse on lovely hours so swiftly flown,
Even yield to recollection its most darling boon.

LXXXIII.

How he made tragedy to strike the heart,
In characters of blood, or dauntless love!
The agonizing Œdipus! we start!
Sorrows, like serpents, round him themselves wove.
Murderer of his father! what can more move?
Seducer of his mother! what more dread?
Loathed by his offspring, marked by gods above,
Another Cain! from mankind's roofs he fled;
The bleak world, with two wretched daughters, doomed
to tread.

LXXXIV.

See the fierce maniac lance his rolling eyes,
From whence, like mountain-streams, pours gory sleet;
Prostrate he reels, as if from heaven's high skies
Hurled headlong earthward by the lightning's shoot!
Hark! Theban corridores clang with his feet;
He bursts the cord that hangs the suicide;
His orbs a mangled wife and mother meet!
He shouts out loud! and, as on whirlwinds, glide
His shrieks through the imperial palace, far and wide.

LXXXV.

Mark too the attachment of Antigone,
Her most heroic love, her firmness' might:
There is in her a grand sublimity
Of elevated feeling! Though 'twas right
To loathe his deeds, yet kept she e'er in sight
The thought he did them all in ignorance.
Affection's constancy in her shone bright;
Of wrong and right possessing such keen sense,
She comes to us in beautiful magnificence!

LXXXVI.

Like a Bœotian morn, upon that night
Of painful darkness, of amazing gloom;
A seraph, robed in clear cerulean light,
Consoling Œdipus in his dark doom.
Such wondrous picture this, there is no room
For further illustration; and the theme
Is quite exhausted; that not only some,
But all, the idea of highest order deem:
The Didascaliæ registered no grander dream

LXXXVII.

Of Fancy's boundless energy! The whole
Delineated too in such a way,
That even it can pierce the schoolboy's soul;
Who yawns while viewing heaven's most proud mid-day
Pictured upon the leaf in strong array,
The mind's description. Yet oft as he reads
A mortal's poignant anguish in this play,
His bosom, which ne'er bled before, now bleeds;
His youthful pulse throbs wildly, pitying such sad deeds.

LXXXVIII.

Past are times spent in porticoes and groves,
When classic heroes dwelt on subjects great;
No more their free almighty genius roves;
Nor tragedy makes canopies of state
Shake with kings' movements as they seemed to await
The glorious actors on the magic stage!
Those days are past: and paltry plays, which grate
Upon the ear, the vulgar herd engage—
So much for this refinement of the present age.

LXXXIX.

Scion of Tragedy! as now we scan
Thy works abounding with celestial grace,
Which shew what dignity belongs to man,
We feel how futile is our highest praise.
'Mid all those monuments that Greece can raise,
The hundred thousand statues to record
Her lords and masters; still we love to gaze
Amid that mighty throng at thine, averred
By all to be of those whose fame is widest heard.

XC.

Argos! upon thy now deserted plain
Theatres in hoary ruins still exist.
Oh! shall we never more behold again
Thy dramas—are such treasures ever missed?
The wandering tribes in fancy stay to list;
The Arachnæan mountains heave with grief;
The breezes, which for thousand years have kissed
Their heavenlike summits, mourn the Avenger's strife;
Ah! sorrowfully moan, refusing all relief.

XCI.

The birds about those hills of beauty fly,
And seem lamenting as they shriek aloud;
Darting adown their chasms with awful cry,
Or soaring upward in the rushing cloud!
Yet seem the Arachnæan ridges proud;
They stand like conquerors, with them Argos pleads;
Their high peaks change, amid the sun, to blood,
As if they frowned on Khalif Omar's deeds,
Whose ruthless disposition would stain Moslem's creeds.

XCII.

I hint not here through him we lost such prize;
But, Science wounded, casts the whole of blame
On that foul traitor. 'Neath Tanagra's skies
Vestiges meet me with immortal name.
Would that ten myriads had been given to Fame,
Illustrious armies battling in her cause;
Then never could such works have felt the shame
Of mouldering into ashes: o'er their stores,
Britain's arenas might have shaken with applause.

XCIII.

Æschylus and Sophocles some so adore,
Euripides they scorn. Not wrong to think
That many a youthful student loves him more;
Though minds matured their taste and feeling link
With Æschylus and Sophocles. I drink
With rapture from his fountain; and I own
That Tasso's sweetness would near such lines sink;
Boccaccio's spirit heave a dying groan;
And Ariosto's grand variety be outdone!

XCIV.

Sometimes, we grant, he passes by some rules,
And for wild splendour fails to be precise;
As widely-ranging fancy half unschools
The laws of accuracy, wondrous nice.
Pressure of images became his choice,
Perhaps was faulty, being out of place;
Yet exquisite-like did the Muses' voice
Speak in his folio, though such crimes we trace,
That his are lines of worth which nothing shall efface.

XCV.

Upon a glittering throne a monarch sate,
Whose costly drapery shone richly gay;
From whence he viewed his navies move in state
Through ocean's grand domain, too great to say—
A terribly magnificent array!
Young concubines smiled round him with the power
Of Houris glittering in celestial day;
Their eyes were lavished, sweet as sunshine shower,
Upon the sceptred king, whose brow with clouds did lower.

XCVI.

On the dread world of sea they seemed withal
An overpowering dawn emerging far;
Gorgeously solemn! whose proud light did fall
On Salamis; which, like a blazing spar,
Reddened the waters. Crimson flags of war
Were the fierce morn, bright galleys were the sun,
Whose right on earth such pageant did now mar.
A stream of glory did before them run,
Whose startling brilliancy the eyes of man might shun!

XCVII.

This august mass of moving empire veered
Towards Salamis; where armies staring stood
Equipped, as spears of brass on high appeared.
The ocean rolled one fiercly-burnished flood!
And rising forms in eastern costume wooed
The fearless eyes of the undaunted Greeks;
Who, like a tempest in determined mood,
Stood firm to overwhelm the unearthly streaks
Of this intruding sun, whose power the mind ne'er speaks.

XCVIII.

Themistocles this boasting despot met;
Beheld his pompous banners strew the shore;
They sank beneath the sea-weed, and there wet
With blood of hundreds, lay in horrid gore!
And nothing ever pleased my boyhood more
Than to reflect when Greece was ever glad;
When Fortune deigned, from out her changing store,
With palms of victory her brow to clad.
Thus often sang I of that fleet in death's dark shade.

1.

Like the waves of great Biscay, when, burnished with gold,
The bright morning shines on them in fulness of power,
Were the galleys and barges of Xerxes outrolled,
That the light of the world 'neath their beams seemed to lower!

2.

While the huge brazen spears bristled tall in the air,
And the shields and acinaces dread notice won;
How they burned on the deep with a fierce giant glare,
Encountering the flash of the flame-breathing sun.

3.

Ye might trace the long streamers the blue ocean dyeing,
Persia's proud eagle floating 'neath Fortune's gay smile;
Ye might trace lovely standards in heaven far flying,
The rich beams from whose colours tinged Salamis' isle.

4.

See the weak-minded monarch regarding his fleets,
Placing absolute trust in mere tinselled array!
Can he know that his gold-armoured thousands are
cheats,
And that courage, not numbers, give nations the day?

5.

But when Evening had wound round fam'd Salamis sea,
Her meek halo of more than a daily serene;
Oh! she could not one fair-gilted galley descry,
For a Xerxes' thick hosts were no more to be seen.

XCIX.

And where wert thou upon the illustrious eve,
That eve thy native island was so blest?
Not yet taught by life's miseries to grieve,
A parent's bosom thy ambrosial rest.
How sunset glistened on the ocean breast!
Persia hung down her head, but Greece smil'd sweet.
Such was that day thy mother first caressed
Her infant, born for many a splendid feat;
A well-remembered day penn'd in the book of Fate.

C.

Hail, comic muse of Aristophanes!
Who drained the very fountain-depths of wit;
How admirably well he seemed to please
Thalia, for her gay wings used to flit
Within his fancy's field so clearly bright.
Sarcastic eloquence flowed out in floods;
Poetic fire, which shed an angry light,
Oft sparkled forth; but not like that which broods
In men of self-tormenting minds, and hateful moods.

CI.

Though comical—commanding is his style;
Though witticisms so glimmer on his pages,
Yet a stern meaning in them could revile,
Far more than tongue, the heroes of those ages.
The critic of his time! at him the sages
Trembled; near him a Cleon did revolt,
One whom "profanum vulgus" e'er engages.
O Aristophanes! the heaviest dolt
Feared the least flash from thy satiric thunderbolt!

CII.

Ye isles of Greece, how worshipped in these days!
When the sweet galaxy shines on your coast,
And Pelops' region drinks its blinking rays,
The traveller here musing is quite lost
In soul-o'erwhelming beauty. There, their boast,
Fighting against the Turkish banners, fell;
Though not a countryman, of him the most
They make. Oh! here the bosom's tide can swell!
For ocean, mounts, and vales, of him their story tell.

CIII.

O Missolonghi! when a Byron died,
When Death made Fame deliver up her son;
When the Muse recognized her Star of pride
Reeling from its high orbit, life's race run;
Then set 'neath Europe's brow another sun;
At once triumphant Glory felt the blow!
Another child of her's its goal had won,
And shed a farewell smile on things below;
But none like Græcia and her islands felt that woe!

CIV.

The wreath of this world's trophies ceased to bloom
Around that noble brow, when Byron's mind
Rocked wild on knowing the unaltered doom
Pronounced by Fate emerging from behind
The drop-scene of Eternity! We find
A deep impression stamped upon those shores
Of his great footsteps, as we calmly wind
O'er Delphi's and Morea's faded stores,
Where the lone pilgrim still that youthful bard deplores.

CV.

O Science' child! we weep upon thy dust,
Hallowed by nations, loved by empires great:
We leave thy ashes sleeping, with the trust
Thou didst repent of actions thousands hate.
Let us not harshly judge the fallen state
Of Genius' scion, dreadly used by Time;
When young in years, but old in griefs, dark Fate
Eclipsed that hopeful sun of light sublime,
Which rose in Albion, set in Missolonghi's clime.

CVI.

Did England nurse her bard—did Albion treat
That outcast wanderer with maternal love?—
Ask the existing race. Blue ocean's sheet
Looked on him as an exile forced to rove,
And seek in foreign lands that tear to move
He could not wrest from Britain's angry heart.
She may have acted right. In realms above
His spirit hopes at length. But I must part
With themes that might be mark for *ignorant* critics' dart.

CVII.

Yet notwithstanding all the foibles of
This most eccentric generation's race,
Has Byron's intellect had strength to move
His worst despisers, though in much disgrace.
The uncommon energy which one can trace
In every line, has caused them to forgive
The offender, and to change their curse to praise.
Though men for most refined summits strive,
In many a hostile library his works shall live.

CVIII.

Adieu, great Byron, evermore adieu!
Horrid to witness thy low-sunken form,
By Death's shaft swept from the empyrean's view,
Where oft thy soul rose grander than the storm!
Thy glorious ashes still appear half warm
With tints of life: the Greek can scarce believe,
As he bends o'er thee, that Fate could so calm
Thy once-impassion'd spirit. Our tears leave
A running fountain at thy tomb; we love to grieve!

CIX.

I dreamed upon an immemorial rock:
Lovely the sea which lay in sleep beneath;
No murmur audible of billows' shock;
Even a painful stillness, like to death;
Not the most gentle breeze emitted breath.
Heroic spirits seem to rise from rest,
And dark green laurels did their pale brows wreath;
Unlike to common shades, they looked quite blest;
In angels' snow-white fair attire they all were dressed.

CX.

Sappho, in youthful loveliness arrayed,
Stood near that queen of stars we all well know;
Her eyes upon her native Greece were staid,
And darkly black as ever did they glow!
Her pallid cheeks were white as drifted snow,
Her brow was beautiful as when on earth;
A cloud of silver glitter'd clear below,
A footstool for her feet. Thus stepping forth,
Stood she as stately as Eve in primeval birth.

CXI.

And Æschylus and Sophocles appeared,
Then stayed with Sappho by the radiant star;
And soon another spirit these three near'd,
Tiresias it was, from heaven afar;
They seem'd a mutual sympathy to share.
O'er Athens Sappho lent her fairy neck,
She pointed to where Cynthia's moonbeams cheer
The palace-halls of Otho, with pale streak;
The dew-drop left her eyes, for Græcia was a wreck!

CXII.

To this celestial group another came,
His noble aspect of the highest sort,
Who sailed to them upon the moonlight flame,
And buried was he in profoundest thought—
Euripides still with stern wisdom fraught.
All stood as friends, their enmities were o'er:
Alas, that land, that land! a thing of nought,
Formed their attention : how they did deplore!
They view'd all from Parnassus to the voiceless shore.

CXIII.

A holiness spread light around that group.
I never felt before as then I felt;
A scene with which a Titian's art might cope;
And to the god-like images I knelt.
Their attitudes made my hard heart to melt!
The nymph of admiration Sappho shone!
Wisdom to Sophocles' fine forehead dealt
Inimitable glory. Seemed each one
Like polished smooth-carved statues of the marble stone.

CXIV.

They stood with an angelic elegance.
I look'd upon these five a moment's time,
When through the horizon's strong magnificence,
In a gay chariot modelled fairly slim,
Of starlight, quite unutterably sublime,
Came Pindar, on whom Sappho sweetly smiled,
Her black eyes sparkled, looking upon him;
Then for a second-like she mildly veil'd
Her face with a star-beam; which was so undefiled.

CXV.

Then shot a spangling lyre along the sky,
Which stripling cherubs bore upon their wings,
Whose radiant brilliancy great heaven did dye!
Of beaten gold gleamed its well-ordered strings;
Its stand was burnished gilt—a beam which brings
Such pretty rays in glimmering paths along.
Memory e'en still to its appearance clings.
Sappho's white fingers roam'd its chords among,
While Pindar seemed to sing with joy the following song:

1.

"There shine some isles in ocean's bright,
Round which sea-breezes blow;
Unutterably grand delight
Their children ever know!

2.

The islands of the blest they are,
Where Hebe loves to roam,
And quaff this pure, this fragrant, air
That fans her radiant home!

3.

Clear skies, of an eternal blue,
O'er-arch these glorious isles;
And Beauty, in undying hue,
Through endless ages smiles!

4.

From them the Paphian land of mirth
Is 'mid its blue deep seen,
Where Cytheræa gained her birth
On ocean's rich serene.

5.

They overlook fair Ida's hill,
Whose smiling summits shine;
Troy in its ruins, sadly still,
Is deemed by them divine!

6.

They mark that spot on Helle's tide,
When furious howls the storm;
Even where Leander calmly died,
His eyes on Hero's form!

7.

And Sestos too is viewed by them,
When Neptune's rampant surge
Tells of that old, that well-known theme,
As whirlwinds heaven's clouds urge.

8.

I know not other isles so sweet
As those sweet isles above;
I know not where calm waters meet
In such transcendent love!

9.

Well I remember when I sought
These isles on earth—what bliss!
Borne in the floods of dreamy thought,
I saw such scene as this.

10.

The blue skies oped one cloudless day,
And shewed me heaven in power!
A flower, fast by a fountain's way,
Poured beams in golden shower.

11.

I passed the mighty ones of heaven,
(My eyes might have seemed rude,)
But all the world I would have given
To 'have called mine this bright bud.

12.

They say this flower for ages burns
To please the immortals' sight,
Which vainly cruel Winter yearns
To blast with icy might!

13.

If Gigas, on his mountains piled,
Had burst heaven's palace gates;
Then would this flower no more have smiled,
Thus crushed by furious Fates.

14.

But now how peaceful it remains!
Its blossoms fresh and new;
More bright than amaranthine veins,
More loved than violet's blue!

15.

Where does it grow? where does it bloom?
In yonder blessed isles!
A brilliant sunshine drives off gloom,
No blight its leaves defiles.

16.

The islands of the blest are glad,
Though other regions frown;
No one in these can say, "I 'am sad,"
For pangs of Fate have flown.

17.

For there the gods a rapture bring,
There goddesses hold sway;
And spirits fly with star-wreathed wing
In everlasting day!

CXVI.

It seemed to me, when Pindar's tones did leave
The silvery air, that Sappho drank Love's draught:
Ye might have seen most gloriously heave
Her broad white bosom! How the dream I quaffed!
It seemed in snowy swellings even to waft
A semblance, like a signal through the air,
That on a lone night hails the seaman's craft;
So beautifully white, so whitely fair,
More exquisite in nakedness, more sweet as bare!

CXVII.

Now Athens for a while forgot her fate,
And listened to the melody. A change
Came o'er her scene. Her fallen towers of state
Rose to perfection wonderfully strange,
As in the days when Freedom used to range
Uninterrupted round her hallowed shore:
Parnassian choruses once more there sang,
And Attica well shone with beauties o'er,
As when decked out so lovely in her dress of yore.

CXVIII.

I saw the classic shades, the Academe,
Beautiful, charming, as they used to be,
When Plato's monstrous energy did beam
With radiance lit from immortality;
The spot, where he reclined, I seemed to see.
I thought the wise man glimmered through the trees,
And held discourses on futurity:
I soon approached the group; a gentle breeze
Fanned the philosopher—to him I bent my knees.

CXIX.

I looked a moment on the harbour blue,
Then turned my path to where the Ilissus winds:
There the most famed Lycæum struck my view,
The school of most incomparable minds.
A spot where Meditation ever finds
A resting place, her memory's will to please;
So aggrandized with relics' various kinds!
One feels, regarding thy grand past, O Greece,
Time's far most favoured tenant has a transient lease.

CXX.

And then the Attic temples lured my gaze,
Piled on tall columns of magnificence;
The emblems of the everlasting days
Of Greece! The moonbeams pouring dense,
Made all more overwhelming to each sense.
And here beheld I true nobility,
As towered to heaven the Acropolis immense!
Near to where Sappho sate upon the sky,
Which pierced the silvery cloud that at her feet would lie.

CXXI.

One thing above all loved I to remark;
I seemed to view the very ancient house
Where Sophocles, inflamed by Wisdom's spark,
Once dwelt and wrote; on whose roofs did repose
The beams of fairy planets in clear rows.
There were the haunts, those glorious haunts of old,
Where, ere the balmy evening sought to close,
He wandered out the aspect to behold,
The famed Piræus glittering in a blaze of gold!

CXXII.

But all this change was only felt by me,
They still saw Athens as it really was;
Fancy is strong in our mortality,
And may be this was the specific cause.
Soon o'er the dreaming scene, a sudden pause!
The eyes of Sophocles seemed sternly bent
Towards the horizon, and the starry doors
Of heaven soft opened, while a vessel leant
Upon the moonlight sea, as from some islet sent.

CXXIII.

It cut the yielding-sky, as if blue ocean;
Oh! 'twas a lovely object to behold!
Its sails were shining silk, which gave it motion,
Its shape the same as oarless skiffs of old.
Hebe, dressed in snow-white well streaked with gold,
Steered it along the circumambient air.
It swept the breeze majestically bold.
Hebe, with her smooth lily ankes bare,
Appeared in heaven an alabaster Venus fair.

CXXIV.

Could ye have seen it slide upon the breeze,
Its merry streamers flapping high and wild,
Doubling the starry capes in airy seas,
Shooting along, by Sappho's eyes beguiled!
Its planks moreover were of gold, defiled
By no foul tarnish; and its glistening deck
Was wrought of ivory, by no dark spot soiled,
As white as Hebe's most angelic neck:
Formed by command divine, no whirlwind could it wreck.

CXXV.

It made for this most interesting group,
O'er Athens vertical. And Sappho chose
To take the silver helm, elate with hope;
In woman's splendour her young figure rose
Unto my dazzled eyes! A sight that woos
The fire in passion's breast! And then I thought
That, being wafted from my rock's repose,
Into this curious vessel I was caught,
To be of Græcia's ancient history better taught.

CXXVI.

It swept along the breeze, I just now said;
For though no breath beneath, it gently blew
In more exalted regions overhead.
Now Sappho with a diamond pencil drew
On crystal glass our route, to nature true.
I felt quite whelmed within this dizzy sphere;
And when to pain astonishment soon grew,
They gave a cordial my faint soul to cheer,
Which half revived my heart, and made my vision clear.

CXXVII.

The grandest sights, the boasts of Greece, I saw!
We passed Ægina's rock, and Salamis;
Then crossed to Sunium's temple now no more;
There pendent over Neptune's calm abyss
We felt the weight of sorrow o'er our bliss.
For such inspiring scenes must yield a joy;
But woe o'er-clouded all. To our fond eyes,
The crescent plains of Marathon, which buoy
The purple cheek of ocean, glittered brilliantly.

CXXVIII.

The moon drooped sadly o'er that silent spot.
"Is this the place," thought I, "which once so rang
With Greece' exploits, my childhood ne'er forgot;
Where with triumphant energy could clang
The warrior's spear and shield: where proudly sang
The Athenians subsequent to victory?
Ah me! ah me! how wonderfully strange
Is it in desolation!" Then a sigh
Was wrung from every breast in depths of agony.

CXXIX.

Now inland further Sappho steered our course
To Decelea's and to Phyle's haunts.
Phyle, that noted spot! where Freedom hoarse
With shouts of gladness made forget their wants
The grief-worn patriots! But stern Justice plants
A stigma, Decelea, upon thy soil;
And though in splendour thy appearance daunts
The pilgrim, wondering at thy cloud-topped pile,
An Alcibiades has darkened thy defile.

CXXX.

The whirlpool of my soul was tumbling with
The swellings turbulent of big ideas!
There is a period that the mind can writhe
Under its own oppression, as it sees
Before it swept, like lightning-blasted trees,
The wreck of all that once was wondrous great!
Yet, Phyle, how thou didst my vision please,
With thy remains of celebrated state,
As I loved in that dream thy form to contemplate.

CXXXI.

Over these mighty passes now we steered
Into Bœotia's fertile, grassy fields;
And well indeed my afflicted mind was cheered
With the green beauty pasturage ever yields;
(Here Nature her most fairy palace builds),
Herds on the hills, within the valleys herds,
And sheep alike. Oh! as the moonbeam gilds
The tinkling streams, it beats description's words,
And to the journeying tribes e'er pleasaunce rich affords!

CXXXII.

But all was opened in a dream to me;
Oh, how romantic did the landscape seem!
The towering tops of mountains could I see
Lined with trees burnished by the nightly gleam;
For Cynthia near earth drove her silvery team.
There in her widowed weeds was Helicon;
The inspirer once of many a joyful theme,
Which strung the harp to a tremendous tone!
But now she was a desolate, a lonely one!

CXXXIII.

And Sappho, dear ideal of loveliness!
Oh! be remembered by me her sad look,
Mixed with enthusiasm's most wild distress,
She gave: at once the glance I could not brook!
The courage of a man my veins forsook.
And Hebe also on that mountain gazed,
Who could not her most poignant anguish cloke.
Tiresias his blue eye of wisdom raised
Towards heaven; alas! the Muses' golden throne was razed.

CXXXIV.

Now skimming through the soft and genial air,
We left Bœotia to her moonlight sleep;
And 'mid this upper atmosphere so rare,
Continued our celestial route to keep.
Many a real instruction did we reap
As gliding over each still sacred scene;
And thousand lordly thoughts would strongly creep
Within the mind of wonders that have been;
All around Greece was nothing but a sweet serene.

CXXXV.

On, on we flew! the fairy streamers waved;
The silk sails gently swelled with breezes mild;
The goddess of the night a fair path paved,
Of burnished silver, wholly undefiled.
Now soon my anxious vision was beguiled
By mountains towering to the horizon far!
At first I deemed it a deserted wild,
Which man to cultivate would never dare;
Tip-toe upon their peaks there stood a blinking star.

CXXXVI.

With horror was my every feeling-struck!
Delphi, the wondrous Delphi! famed of old,
Born in that country doomed to such ill-luck,
Aghast shrunk 'neath my gaze! Ye might behold
Declivities quite rocky, steeps high rolled
Together. I now spied 'mid one recess
A chapel in the light its form unfold,
A crucifix upon its top. A press
Of many heavy thoughts shot through my soul distress.

CXXXVII.

"Spot once of Liberty, of Life, of Love!
Where is thy temple of Apollo now,"
(For thus I reasoned gazing from above,)
"Which shed renown round great Parnassus brow,
That made Castalia's streams more purely glow?
Where thy three thousand statues so sublime;
What awful monster struck with deathly blow
Their grandeur, grandest 'neath the roof of Time?
What could repay for such a fierce enormous crime?

CXXXVIII.

"There's not one stone to tell me of thy fate;
There's not one noble column of that pile;
No lovely relic speaks thy better state,
When thou could'st like a cheerful angel smile
Viewing thy shrine piled up to heaven's tall hill.
I see some lone trees planted here and there;
But these no doubt are younglings of the soil,
Which cannot to my ear the tidings bear
Of thy magnificence thus hurled to deep despair!

CXXXIX.

"Ah! Delphi no more listen to the prayers
Breathed from the bosom of the wandering Greek;
There was an hour when thou didst heal the cares
Of those through their dear country's sorrows weak.
They could their mind to thee in boldness speak.
Then to thy shrine the solemn tribes did come,
And left their native pastimes for thy sake;
Here from far distant regions would they roam
From many a foreign shore, from many an island home!

CXL.

"Thus lies great Delphi! stripped of every glory;
Its mountains desolate—its shrine no more.
On her lone waste the shepherd tells his story,
And thrills the listener to the bosom's core;
Even eighteen hundred years and forty-four,
Stop! let me think; yes, even more, I rue!
Since her renowned and matchless structures bore
Man's heart and soul away. And now we view
The waste, waste site, which seems to thunder forth—
"adieu!"

CXLI.

"Ah me! oh! Sappho burst this awful spell,
To eye yon Delphi is a painful thing;
The billows of the soul, like high hills swell,
And on the mental shore with vengeance ring,
Louder than those loud sounds which tempests bring!"
No sooner had I uttered these last words,
Than Sappho spread the vessel's silken wing,
And passed we over some barbarian hordes
Sleeping in tents beneath. Such change the scene affords.

CXLII.

Dreams must for ever some strange sight contain:
I thought where'er in our smart bark we went,
On the blue bosom of the ethereal plain
That star, I saw at first, above us leant,
Just like a guardian cherub, as intent
To save us from a fall precipitate:
And when the Delphian waste made all give vent
To maddening floods of anguish, and of hate,
I saw its orb expand and gild sad Phocis' state!

CXLIII.

If I proceeded fully to display
The every scene that aggrandized my dream,
'Twould make a copious book. Suffice to say
How beautifully sad each spot must seem!
Reviewing such, anon the flickering gleam
Of a most unexampled past revived;
Temples and relics in the moonlight beam,
Which in their sunken attitudes still grieved,
Though not of autour, and their dignity, bereaved.

CXLIV.

Thus to sail round Greece by the lonely night,
When the moon with her silvery pen retraces
On blue leaves of the sky with letters bright
Great Athens, Corinth, and the illustrious places
Almost bereft of all their ancient graces,
Perhaps is solemn, yet a grand pursuit!
Here where the glittering chariots ran their races,
Here where unequalled armies made their route!
Whatever blends with memory's responding note.

CXLV.

All rush again in one o'ercoming flood!
While we look on them e'en as exiles look
The last time on their country; and the blood
Of passion, feeling, woe, that none can brook,
Mounts, like a torrent, in their bosom's nook.
Thus gaze we upon Greece! her voiceless coast,
Her land all round, sleep calm beneath the stroke;
Soft sighs she for those heroes ever lost,
Where on her dying shores Fame's sun-set makes its boast!

CXLVI.

But to proceed. The dream now waxes dim;
They placed me once more on the silent rock,
Then rose in air; my eyes began to swim;
I felt a tremor, then a sudden shock.
The fairy vessel did most sweetly rock:
The sky appeared bright, like an ocean blue,
A distant sparkling sea; they softly broke
Its liquid surface, 'till their figures grew
Half indistinct. I rose to wave one last adieu.

CXLVII.

And in the anxious struggle I awoke.
I started up scarce able to believe.
Oh! could I but describe the anxious look,
When I no more could their sweet forms perceive!
I eyed the far sky round: how did I grieve,
When I felt 'twas a vision in my sleep,
And nothing more: I made a spring to dive
Within the sweet, calm heaven—a futile leap—
Then angry, discontented, sate I down to weep.

CXLVIII.

Fancy my consternation when appeared
Athens in ruined grandeur! in its streets
Some lonely stranger walked, who almost feared
His death as looking there; each one he meets
He eyes with caution, and with distance greets
All passers by. Upon the Acropolis
Some base intruders dwelt on ancient feats;
And now they spake of her illustrious rise;
And now they spake of such destruction of her bliss.

CXLIX.

Shine, Athens shine, in all thy pristine strength!
I would a Grecian Marcus Curtius be,
Nor halt upon the gulph, whatever length,
But to restore thy past celebrity!
Where is the chasm? No chasm shall hinder me,
Though monsters from it wind above the clouds,
And hiss in thunderstorms! And e'er I die,
Even as sinking down, the cave's dark shrouds,
"Victory!" will I cry to thy o'er-gazing crowds!

CL.

O Greece, the fairest charm of boyhood's days!
Like a sweet mermaid glittering on the ocean,
Thy sea-cliffs smote the heart with Beauty's rays,
And seemed to move along in queen-like motion.
History could not inspire one glorious notion,
If Greece, Greece's beauties, and Greece's victories
Had dormant lain. And though Death's bitter potion
Has chilled thy passionate heart; yet still surprise
Love, admiration, each such power us to *thee* ties.

CLI.

And now I am compelled with thee to part
For other classic lands, the abodes of Fame;
But thou shalt still be nearest to my heart,
A school-boy worshipped I thy glorious name!
And though in Granta's haunts, yet still the same
My deep affection for thee never fades;
And as I muse again on childhood's dream,
When oft in thought I wandered 'neath thy shades,
My tears burst copious forth,and memory their flow aids.

CLII.

O Greece! the dearest joy my heart has known,
In all the spring-tide of its blooming year,
Has soonest taken wings, and swiftest flown,
To leave me isolated, friendless, here.
A ship-wrecked mariner on some waste sphere
I seem, in vain deploring all my gloom;
The ships I hail, in vain I drop the tear,
They pass me by in ocean's awful room;
Then let me perish thus, my friends lie in the tomb.

CLIII.

And I shall only die to be with them.
Oh! this is bliss! though cold in their abode;
Yet what can Love's unbridled torrent stem?
Their absence is the intolerable load!
The sting of dreadful scorpions cannot goad,
The spear of rude barbarians cannot pierce,
The frame so fearfully. The gloomy mood
Of disappointed love scowls far more fierce
Than any form that Sorrow wears on Death's dark
hearse.

CLIV.

In Greece the Muses' strains are heard no more,
In Greece the voice of poetry is fled;
The Epinician odes we now deplore,
And Tragedy's last beam of fire is shed.
Yet Fame's light gilds the face of Græcia's dead,
Which Raphael's glorious pencil could not paint,
Though 'twas unearthly, godlike! And her head
Shines still with Glory's crown, though dim and faint;
Oh! never shall she History's best encomiums want!

CLV.

And now, my lyre, I bid thee sleep awhile,
My fingers shall calm rest upon thy strings;
'Tis his to weep in duty, not to smile,
Who of the greatest nation's ruin sings.
And, resting here, fond imitation clings
To minstrels' ways in happier times of old;
Who in grand towers were listened to by kings:
These often stemmed the fiery theme to unfold,
With stronger pomp and power, the legends that they told.

END OF CANTO I.

INTRODUCTION TO CANTO II.

TO NATURE.

WHAT see I glistening in her native wilds,
Deer and fawns by her side; empyreal roses
Around her brow; on couch which Phœbus gilds,
Her elegant, her royal form reposes?
'Tis Nature! by her grassy bed there oozes
A wondrous lucid fountain; and a lamb
Sips up the crystal drink; and, quite free, chooses
To leave man's works for Nature's tranquil calm;
Now nibbles it the grass, which smells like fragrant balm.

My very childhood worshipped at thy shrine,
Fair-featured Nature. School-books thrown aside,
The green, green meads attired in flowers divine,
The silent flow of some sweet river's tide,
Invited me; the towering mountains dyed
In hues of evening's radiance my soul thrilled.
Hither, remote from mankind, oft I hied;
And though with gushing tears my eyes were filled,
The tears of contemplation such; which helped to gild

My future prospects; as, with anxious eye,
I looked into Futurity's abyss;
And in its chasm of immortality,
Painted beyond this world a home of bliss.
Unfathomed are thy beauties; for there is
A splendour inexpressible in thee,
Great Nature; so that what high sovereigns prize,
Dominion, man's applause, formality,
Compared with thy vast kingdom, seem but vanity.

I ask no lovelier, sweeter sky of morning,
I ask no purer gleam thine that at night,
I ask no grander clouds to give the warning
Of the terrific coming tempest's might;
I ask no more august and thrilling sight
Than the fierce lightning! No! there is no fault
In Nature's framework—all, yes, all is right:
And as the rattling thunder shakes heaven's vault,
I stand to hear the omen, with surprise I halt!

Nature! clasp round the girdle of thy seasons,
Spring, summer, autumn, winter, come with me
To fertile climates, where Hyperion's sons
Ride in rose-tinted chariot o'er the sea.
Or to the valleys of Cashmere which see
The dates and palm trees brightning 'neath the sun;
Minarets glittering like eternity;
Maids with the raven hair, which Phœbus shun:
Lying in gilded homes round which cool waters run.

If such can't be, yet waft me from this hum
Of Thames-oppressing commerce to some spot,
Where glad hills yield a contrast to the scum
Of a "profanum vulgus:" fix my lot
In rude ravines where gleams the shepherd's cot;
Where dingles ring with melody of birds;
Lowing and bleating I ne'er yet forgot;
And glimmering thro' the trees the flocks and herds
By rushing mountain cascades; scene that beggars words;

That beggars Fancy in its truth to picture;
So wildly rural! yet the throne of Love;
Of roughness, and magnificence, a mixture;
Torn rocks, and shaggy steeps, o'er which there rove
The untamèd bounding elks; which, as a dove,
Quite harmless, and quite mortal-fearing, are.
'Tis in such glorious haunts that man can prove
The soul's grand boundlessness; when, as in war,
The feelings and the passions strive for heights afar;

That, like huge battlements, one overtower
With Chimborazo majesty; built up
By Nature, not with trouble, but with power,
Even by a "Let there be!" Proud men, low stoop,
As ye stand exercising your vain hope
That ye can work the same; vain worms, avaunt!
The labour of a day will make *you* droop;
Ye then hang down your heads, so weak, so faint;
Ye are too feeble, one cannot that weakness paint.

Behold revolving round the shades of night!
The sheep are bleating, for they seek their fold;
The sapient dog, with wondrous wisdom dight,
Can now afar the evening star behold.
The scene is very beautiful unrolled!
He now barks loud, and drives the anxious flock;
While the West glitters in its last fair gold.
Round mountains, over streams, and moistened rock,
He urges them along—the woods his barkings mock.

The lowing herds too lie them down to rest,
They have no fold, nor shingle-roofèd bed;
But, on the earth's unsheltered dewy breast,
They chew the cud and sleep, from all care freed.
These nibble in night's noon the thistle weed,
When most luxurious starlight bursts like day,
And wakens them all up, once more to feed;
While the young moon-beams on the green grass play—
Is there a more delightful scene? Enthusiast, say!

Once more behold the shepherd light his lamp,
The lattice drink the entertaining rays.
As Hope's soft light within the ethereal camp,
Star-like it cheers the pilgrim's pathless ways.
'Tis brighter to him than the mid-day blaze
Along yon proud empyrean! here he hies.
The shepherd's charity no cheat betrays,
He shares his all with him, his best supplies;
Down at the stranger's feet is laid his chiefest prize.

One tells unto the other some sweet tale,
Whose hero and fair heroine were of yore;
Whose characters would ne'er be flat and stale,
Reiterated though even o'er and o'er.
On legend humble life e'er loves to pore;
And thus they soothe away the vacant time,
Till they have nigh exhausted all their store;
Then with thy calm, Repose, their tired limbs chime;
Their night dreams conjure up rich thoughts of days sublime.

The lion is more true than worldly man,
Androcles saw superior mind has he;
Such court your favour no more than ye can
Afford to indulge the pomp of luxury.
But when the lion once again did see
His Androcles; although a victim made,
His dreadful paws stood still; his fiery eye
Looked on him like a lamb; his jaws were staid!
Oh, say how sweetly was this gratitude repaid!

I read the story when a little child,
Admired the kingly lion's gratitude;
When from the savage hungred he turned mild,
Even as the faithful dog; his aspect rude
Changed in a moment to love's radiant mood!
This is a story, but the moral's true;
We have beheld the wild beast from the wood
Act nobler than the mass; even though a few
There evermore exist, who shall redeem our crew.

Men in a mean condition are oft better
Than the most gorgeous-attired sovereigns;
The latter so contented with the letter,
Formality gets blended with their veins.
The former, led by Nature's simple reins,
Have artless yet pure motives to induce
Action's performance. In such bosoms reigns
Serenity so genial, so profuse;
Fair are the suns which shine upon the road they choose.

Nature! the ruddy cheek, the eye of joy,
Glittering amid the clear, chill air; the spell
Of raptures which the poor swain's spirit buoy,
Speak of a peaceful mind, a young heart well.
Around yon village hearth red cheeks will tell
This night of comfort monarchs never had.
The mother, at the sound of evening's bell,
That last of sunny day when all seem glad,
Meets her child plodding through the fields, no more is sad.

Now as the sunset streaks the Winter sky,
The ploughboy, homeward bending, fancy feeds;
He views through trees his bright hut with his eye,
Seems as if empires his, and feels no needs.
Round him are undulating vales, and meads,
Where life's most busy scenes appear quite slow
Departing with the sun; he joyful reads
His fate in clouds which, like vermilion, glow;
Sees the horizon's crimson tinsel hills of snow.

How beautiful, how more than sweet, to him
The soft scenes of the evening appear;
When through his lowly mind there often swim
Ideas which to a big colossus rear
Themselves: exalting him unto a sphere
Beyond conception's pencil to relate.
Oft he considers Nature quite severe,
Awarding sovereigns such a care-worn state;
For happy, oh, how happy is the ploughboy's fate!

Times there are when Heaven's gracious windows ope,
Well showering with resplendent beams the minds
Of the most humble; and the blaze of hope
Turns to more radiant colours when it finds
An entrance in such breasts. The pompous blinds,
That windows overhang of kings' saloons,
Too oft shut out the light that so reminds
The pilgrims of the days that have no noons;
Which, glittering fair with endless suns, need no pale moons.

Oh! see around the straw-thatched hut that gleam
Which even the rays of palace splendour mars.
Contentment's halo glistening, like some dream,
Calm-shining, far from man's intestine wars,
No revelry at night! The smiling stars
Mark, sitting happy on his wooden stool,
By the gay blaze, the ploughboy; who now shares
Village amusements which delight his soul.
Not the poor man, the rich man oftener is Grief's tool!

Say not what men have done, what they can do;
Away with warriors' military deeds,
Nor be to earth's unnoticed ones untrue;
For popular heroes mere to esteem as weeds
The pauper's pious acts, his practised creeds!
Even in his lonely hut, at midnight's hour,
Fame's most ambitious lamp at seasons sheds
Around his lowly mind the exciting shower;
As wonderful chimeras flamed him with their power!

Misfortune quenched them. And the plough-boy's soul
Felt, but a moment, pride's indignant sting;
Contentment's narrow home, her wooden stool,
Her grateless fire, still life's chief comforts bring.
Oh! in thy humble cell forbear to wring
Thy hands in anguish, stripling more than blest;
I tell thee, monarchs in night's hours would fling
Their costly robes away to have thy rest,
To feel upon their bed of state thy happy breast.

What matters their display of regal show;
The purple curtains, and the gorgeous quilt,
The golden borders as they loosely flow,
The body of the couch inlaid with gilt?
What matters? For too oft the burnished hilt
Of Fear's sword glitters on the broidered pillow,
Fast by the jewelled crown; and oft is spilled
In cushioned sleep his blood. Yes, one hears through
Their bosom the heart heaving like a maddened billow!

Now shines the morning on the earth again,
The stripling leaves his beautiful repose;
He opes his lattice; then pours in the strain
Of little winter birds that calm the woes
Of most desponding hearts. Ah! thus he knows
Felicity dwells not with stingy wealth;
That pompous battlements increase the throes
Of polished minds which weep in chamber stealth;
Then he compares their languor with the plough-boy's
health.

Let kings behold him yoke his freshened team!
Let kings behold the joy his features wear!
Then see him plod along, 'mid some sweet dream
Of the young damsel whom he deems most fair;
With whom in future years he hopes to share
His well-earned substance, what is more, his heart:
Not wedded, like some fashionable pair,
For money's sordid gains; whence soon depart
Domestic charms, whence each through lifetime feels
grief's smart.

He drives his team around the base of hills,
Where icicles on trees, in silvery bands,
Usurp their thrones; where warrior rills
Wage a loud battle with the pebbled sands.
He ploughs fields, which, when touch'd with Summer's
hands,
Paint the declivities of mountain sides,
As if transformed to such by Genii's wands:
And while Time's changing chariot onward glides,
He marks its warning scenes in all their various tides.

This happy swain wears out life's transient dream
In yon vale where his native village lies;
Where winding round it Anio's ancient stream
The pilgrim from a weeping Rome espies.
What! shall the scholar scornfully despise
The poor plough-boy, because his station low?
How can we tell his genius did not rise
Loftier than Mantua's scion, until the blow
Of ruthless Poverty stemmed Science in its flow?

CANTO II.

I.

Ye intellects, of this high-learned day!
Ye critics! who presume to judge the rhyme,
Ye yourselves know as much about as they,
Who oft on Pegasus with madness climb:
But ere he attains the first stage of his prime,
And paws the big clouds of the rampant storm,
They tumble downward from heights so sublime
Mangled most terribly in face and form,
The yelling Furies, in wild postures, round them swarm

II.

Italia! loveliest realm the mind to feast;
Thy marble palaces, thy glittering halls,
Adorned with *modern* beauties, Fancy's taste;
Thy gulph of Venice, which in grandeur falls
Upon the eye; thy terraces and walls
So beautifully splendid, would draw tears
From any mortal's soul. And he who hails
Thee gay, outdecked with isles and famous spheres,
And in thy seas with sweet maids for thy gondoliers,

III.

Weeps now; but they are tears of awful sorrow,
Thy day's meridian radiance has past by.
Ah! what lost child can say, "Upon the morrow
Shall be restored my ruined Italy!
And once again with glad heart shall I see
Rome, seven-hilled Rome, the mistress of the world;
And hear the captive shout out, 'I am free!'
Emerging from his cell behold unfurled
Italia's banners floating high, on proud gales curled."

IV.

Ruined, though seated in the golden lap
Of monarch-like Magnificence! Alone
Though millions sailed round Leuca's eastern cape,
And, landing on her beach, in triumph shone,
As sweet as Cytheræa's fairy zone:
Widowed, though lordly suitors at her side
Of high ancestral birth, for never won
Can be her heart again; her husband died,
When died the noblest of the Cæsars—Roma's pride!

V.

Even her sea-weeds shine holy to the gaze;
Her shores are beautiful, although a waste
Contrasted with their pomp in ancient days;
Her sands glow rich, though they to ruin haste.
Memento, yes, the loveliest of the past!
Though ruined, yet her cities wear a bloom;
The hectic flush that even Death cannot blast,
That hues the marble cheek in its last doom,
As on a dying charming woman's ere the tomb!

VI.

But why indulge this anguish on the brink
Of sorrowing Italy? It is enough
From dread Distraction's ocean deep to drink
When, past the threshold, we behold the roof
Of her sweet, yet sad, sky. And here aloof,
Standing on these huge mountains, I shall muse.
But ere I enter, I shall give the proof
I eye her with deep passion, nor refuse
Her love that never more its flaming fire shall lose!

VII.

When thousand, many thousand, miles away,
Over the dark blue sea where Summer shines,
Have I looked forward to that glorious day
That I should hail the illustrious Apennines;
And here they tower at last! The moonlight lines
Their peaks with silver tinsel; and starlight
Meets the tremendous hills; nor my soul pines
That, in the voiceless silence of midnight,
I am indulging visions like the eremite;

VIII.

Or that in midnight's overwhelming calm,
These mountains, loved so long, I thus first hail.
No! when the rosy morning yields its balm,
The Apennines, dressed up in gold, shall steal
Upon my eyesight; and if I can feel,
I shall, by such a pageant, be o'ercome.
No exiled patriot shall enjoy more weal,
Returning to his country and his home,
Than I who see you, borne o'er many a wave of foam.

IX.

O long-loved Apennines! am I allowed
At last your darling glorious scenes to greet?
But stop! but stop! I must not speak thus loud,
Or else yon Cynthia in the ethereal sheet
May be disturbed—a whisper is more meet
At such a voiceless, holy hour. I am
Upon the Apennines! O thought, too sweet!
Upon those hills which did my affection claim
In school-boy days. Too sweet, it must be some bright dream!

X.

Oh, no! 'tis not; awake, my heart, awake!
They are the Apennines I now behold!
With all their matchless majesty they break
Upon thee, in their dignity outrolled.
Never, no, never could a dear friend fold
Another dear friend to his throbbing breast
More warmly, with a passion never told,
Than I (and witness it, thou Heaven at rest),
Who now embrace these mountains, in the deed so blest.

XI.

Am I deemed an enthusiast, because
Love, glory, admiration, ardour, raise
My bosom's fervency? I stand! I pause!
Remorseless at reproof—flow forth, my praise!
Long, weary, toilsome, billowy, were the ways
My bark of life took ere I reached this spot;
But oh! how I forget those irksome days;
Oh! how in rapture's ecstasy I float,
Swallowed up in the thoughts of this, my happy lot!

XII.

By yon pale moon that gilds such sacred scenes,
By yon sweet planet that keeps envious guard
From Italy to Sicily, one gleans
Inspiring information; not debarred
From Heaven's unmeasured circuit. Quite unmarr'd
By the rough strokes of Time's imperial scythe,
Which mows down empires, these tall mounts appear'd
Some fleeting centuries since; and now so blithe,
So gay appear; and planets sport upon their height.

XIII.

Is it not true, some hundred years ago,
That Hannibal, with his most warlike troops,
Made on these mountains a majestic show
Of this world's pageantry? In pompous groups
They marched, elated with transcendent hopes,
Over these monstrous heights; this warrior
Led them along the Apennines' high tops;
They seemed on War's big crimson wings to soar;
A glittering body shone they, handsome flags they bore;

XIV.

Whatever makes vast armies to look gay,
They had with them; whatever power presumes.
Son of Hamilcar, grand was thy array!
Spears, burnish'd shields, and proudly floating plumes,
Burning as 'twere with glory's wondrous fumes;
Like that wild brilliancy the sun outpours
Upon a scorching day, when it illumes
The sky and earth so fiercely with hot showers!
But who describe in truth thy army's awful powers?

XV.

Son of Hamilcar! from these Apennines
Vainly I now address thy numerous host;
Ah! long since thunder-struck with death it pines
In that world where it never more shall boast.
On the wide waste of the eternal coast,
No "wars or rumours of wars" can there be;
Millions of armies there are easy lost;
Enormous empires are too small to see,
When rolled down this abyss of immortality!

XVI.

See the child watch the golden flies of June,
Merrily making boot on summer flowers;
But when appears the yellow autumn moon
It sees no more these gay tribes; all their stores
Are left for others; vainly it deplores.
O Hannibal! these strangely transient tribes
So clearly typify thy faded powers;
Though they are beautiful, no one describes
How soon their tints decay; how fade their brightest stripes!

XVII.

Ye glittering heaps, that look a moment grand;
Ye emblems of earth's vanity, adieu!
These Apennines, which still in firmness stand,
Call forth from ages' dark abyss to you!
They ask the solemn question; and in view
The quivering lightning pens your wretched fate;
The heavy, heavy clouds rush on anew,
Pour down fierce torrents at a fearful rate,
The dreadful tears they weep upon your last estate!

XVIII.

Ye monstrous bulwarks! o'er whose hilly chains
Imperious phalanxes in power have crossed;
In pomp's parade, with echoing trumpet strains,
To add some other nations to the lost;
To buffet lands by revolution tossed.
Survey these by-gone feats of Hannibal;
O Cannæ! had not Fate his thoughts engrossed,
Roma, its haughty Capitol, its all,
Must then have lain unlaurelled, met its final fall!

XIX.

Musing on war, Napoleon's wondrous works,
The great deeds he accomplished, will salute
Me in the vision's field: though fancy shirks
The mighty task, my lyre will not be mute.
When France became far wilder than the brute
Which shakes the savage desert with his roars;
When she killed many thousands, with ears shut
To Pity's horrid shrieks: then Battle's doors
Were opened hugely wide; on Discord's shaggy shores

XX.

The billows, drunk with blood, did madly roll;
Despair, that hideous monster! left his caves,
In Paris' streets to gorge his hungry soul;
And the Atlantic's mountain-towering waves
Were dyed with his dread feasting. Tombs and graves
Then were dispensed with, and a deep-hewn pit
Was filled with slaughtered forms (the bosom heaves!)
Of women beautiful in dreadful plight;
Angelic corpses, rudely gashed, appalled the sight.

XXI.

O shocking age! the hair would stand on end,
My heart would stagger, if I dwelt upon thee:
But if I am compelled my mind to bend
'Neath duty's yoke, my meditation be
On noblest of these times of agony;
Though these are also fearful in the extreme!
Yet the wide-stretching soul will e'er be free
On such proud elevations; and its dream
Extends with Nature's grandeur. Follow then the theme.

XXII.

'Twas evening on the plains of Waterloo;
The sun glanced wildly on the blazing height
Of heaven; and rushing down the sky's pale blue,
A stream of crimson flashed in grandest might.
The lion, monument of that dread fight,
Lolled on his well-known throne in kingly gait;
His eyes seemed bent upon the western light,
As if some apparition going to await,
Armed heads, the ghosts of warriors moving through
Death's state.

XXIII.

No murmur crept along these stilly plains;
But, sliding on its liquid path, the moon
Mingled its white beams with the sun's red veins:
The effect was gorgeous in the high saloon
Of air and breeze. It was the eighteenth of June;
Twenty-five transient years had rolled along,
Since England's iron hero, on its noon,
Led blue-eyed Peace earth's raging climes among;
Since realms united in the chorus of her song.

XXIV.

I met on those plains, such a bright noon-day,
An old man habited in pilgrim's gown;
His silvery hair adown his shoulders lay
In white profusion, fine as silk well spun.
To his high forehead one curl its way won:
Oh, venerable shone his snowy beard!
His handsome face was deep with wrinkles sown.
With dignified appearance, past all word,
He gently smiled on me, then sighed scarce to be heard.

XXV.

One of the last old veterans who had drunk
On Waterloo the cup of bitterness.
Not the look his of the self-slaving monk,
But troubles sent by God, which made him bless
The sender of them: one might easy guess
Such was the cause of his grief so subdued.
Could ye have seen the radiant gloriousness
Of that eve's sun, just bursting from a cloud;
Even so at intervals his mind peeped through woe's
shroud.

XXVI.

His bright blue eyes did sparkle as he spoke;
But 'twas the flash of memory, not wild joy!
"There was a time," said he, "when morning broke
Upon this fated tract, and its fair eye
Beheld no marks of blood's eternal dye;
Was unsuspecting of War's murderous tread;
Weighed with no battle smoke, it could defy
Far India's ocean clearness. Now have fled,
And fled for ever too, those seasons with the dead.

XXVII.

"The field of battle's a tremendous thing!
The far, hoarse, rumbling noise of martial tide,
The cannon-bolt, borne on Death's gory wing,
The smoky volleys rattling far and wide.
The yells and groans of wounded ones that glide
As on the whirlwind's pinions to your ear;
Stunning sounds of artillery! the tide
Of rushing blood, just from its fountain clear,
Pouring like headlong cataracts downward, far and near.

XXVIII.

"The fine black steeds heroically charge
At the foot regiments in opposing form:
The helmeted dragoons, with weapons large,
Flash on your vision, like the Atlantic's storm.
Yon warrior chief, just now with vengeance warm,
Lies stretched in dying posture on the plain;
A friend kneels near. Endeavouring to be calm,
The wretch, life ebbing-fast, unclasps a chain,
Yields up the portrait of her no more seen again.

XXIX.

"The girl who loves him is far, far away;
But different are her hopes of that dear one.
Thus reasons she: 'Oh! Fortune gilds his day;
The soldier shall return with laurels won;
Then happy shall we meet—the conflict done!'
Conceive her anguish when the tidings come!
Her rosy cheek soon waxes faint and dun;
Each day beholds her hastening to the tomb,
The yielding victim of a disappointment's doom.

XXX.

"Moonlight wept over Mount St. Jean's famed peaks;
The cannon's roll had ceased to shake the air;
And nought was heard save some o'erwhelming shrieks
Of wretches writhing in their last despair.
Some horsemen, on whose brows was printed care,
Were stumbling o'er the corpses of the slain:
The heroic Wellington was one even there;
But his high heart was weeping on that plain:
'I never fought so dread, and may I ne'er again!'

XXXI.

"For thus the gallant warrior sadly spoke,
As he just cast a boundless gaze around,
And saw even thousands prostrate by Death's stroke,
And heard the dying as they madly groaned.
Yet France deserved that ne'er-forgotten wound!
The uncircumscribed ambition, monstrous pride
Of Buonaparte, their end at last had found;
Stemmed was the current of their unmatched tide;
And it had been good had he on these dread plains died.

XXXII.

" I could enlarge my subject—I could paint
War's splendid horror thy young heart to strike!
But I am old, and waxes weak and faint
The lamp of energy; and I'm not like
What once I was, when health's vermilion streak
Burned in my looks 'mid boy-hood's by-gone prime;
When the clear rose of England on my cheek
Blushed bright and vigorous—that's a faded time,
Which shines upon my aged memory yet sublime!

XXXIII.

" Voluminous might be such floods of thought.
One might to endlessness indulge this train;
Depict the heavy woes that war has brought,
From Waterloo, that stained this outstretched plain,
(The worst one we may see for years again)
To Hastings where great Harold's blood was spilled:
But the day is already on the wane;
And, lo! the setting sun begins to gild
The horizon's cornice; and the West with light is filled.

XXXIV.

" Yet one word more. There England's champion stood,
A hero for unequalled actions born;
Napoleon there, that thirster after blood!
The Almighty's scourge to make the world forlorn;
On wings that seemed omnipotent once borne."
Here ceased the old man, for to sorrow grew
His deep emotions; and he seemed quite worn
With long-enduring grief; for once he knew
Far better days, and tears rushed from his eye of blue.

XXXV.

I never shall forget that bright noon-day!
I bade the aged veteran long farewell:
I could with him have ever wished to stay,
And, as if struck with an electric spell,
I traced his tottering figure down a dell,
As it was bending towards the pilgrim's road,
Till my eyes, swimming, on it no more fell.
I thought, as almost paralyzed I stood,
That we should meet no more till risen from the sod!

XXXVI.

Adieu, thou weary pilgrim, still adieu!
Now sinks more strikingly thy farewell glance,
Like that grand sun emitting lovelier hue,
As it is leaving life's most vain expanse.
Adieu! and if good heaven my prayer e'er grants,
Even should we meet no more in time below,
Upon the radiant shore which Pleasure haunts,
The pilgrim and the youth, past mortal woe,
Shall clasp each other's hands, each other ever know!

XXXVII.

But I must cease to wander. I entreat
My mind to ruminate on subjects near;
Themes in themselves so beautiful, so sweet,
The more we dwell upon them, still more dear.
'Twas that great France and Italy appear
To me by similar religion joined,
I dwelt upon the former; I did rear
Many an image in my childish mind
Of Waterloo's fine heroes; thus they entrance find.

XXXVIII.

Even so the trespass will be blotted out,
And by the reader shall I be forgiven.—
But stop! what see I on its fairy route,
O'er the smooth channel of the melting heaven?
It is the two-horned Luna, who is driven
In mild car that has braved unnumber'd storms:
Fairies, from fairy isles, seem to be given
To circle her around in glittering swarms;
Unspeakably transcendent shine their well-shaped forms.

XXXIX.

Royalty, on grand wings, pervades these heights;
Here is the theatre for giant joys;
Volumes of inexpressible delights,
To which man's common pleasures are mere toys!
Behold the effect. How yonder proud cloud buoys
The watchful swain who felt no awe before:
Even more than deadening sleep he now enjoys,
That blazing pageant on the immortal shore,
The radiant Venus tripping blue fields o'er and o'er.

XL.

Like million glow-worms creeping through the sky,
Those glimmering worlds of light move calmly on;
Burnishing earth and heaven with lovely dye,
Advancing tow'rds th' horizon, one by one.
Long upon Gothard's sacred peaks have shone
The beauteous planets, counting their gold beads;
When, in the midnight's most romantic noon,
The convent's walls oft wear the sable weeds
Of meek-eyed Penitence, lamenting daylight's deeds.

XLI.

Heart, soul, consenting, I would gladly stay,
Could I command the eagle's feathery plumes,
Even on these Apennines, where young stars play,
And where the mountain pine so graceful blooms:
Even here where merry moonlight's face illumes
The towering hills, the gulleys dark and deep.
Here too for grandeur; when the tempest booms
Shake the black heaven, and on the large clouds leap,
Just like a mighty Giant starting from his sleep!

XLII.

Pause here! Here contemplate, you must rejoice!
Rearing its haughty summits past the moon,
Afar Mount Blanc emerges; where the voice
Is lost in boundless realms; and where we swoon
With giddiness. 'Tis night's all silent noon;
And a world dignified arises clear;
Heaven's beautiful, and star-inlaid saloon
Smiles cheerful on the far enormous sphere;
Mountains on mountains, dipp'd in moonlight, strike
with fear,

XLIII.

But with fine fear, the breast. O'er a high coast
I sit; while low beneath me ocean, flushed
With paly beams, bursts brighter than bright zinc
Upon the gaze; e'en every wave lies hushed;
And the round sea is by no breakers pushed
Headlong to shore. The horizon's silver meets
The blue and tranquil waters. Heaven has blushed
So exquisitely on one, that there greets
My eye a fairy scene, which mortal pen defeats.

XLIV.

The sea-girt mountains form my Paradise,
However horrible their rugged space,
If the loved spirit, my soul's chiefest prize,
Illumined them with her seraphic face;
If near rude precipices I could trace
The soft blue of that eye I cannot paint,
Exquisite, how delightful! Oh, the mace
Of Time to glorious woman ever grant;
Her rounded arm *must* wield it nobly, though 'tis faint!

XLV.

Woman! the *best* idea that ever came
Within my heart shall willingly be thine;
The *grandest* thought, fired with Ambition's flame,
Shall above all earth's beauties call thee mine!
Of purer clay than man—yes, all divine!
Woman! thou hast much power; at thy fair feet
Emperors, despotically proud, recline;
Forget their dignity, thy charms so sweet,
Forget a moment what they are—O vast defeat!

XLVI.

Woman! thou fatal idol of man's soul!
How Youth's blood mantles, when, approaching nigh
To thee, he sees thy orbs so fiery roll,
Like the twin brothers of the thrilling sky.
Passion is swallowed up in Victory,
And thou the victor! yes, O woman, thou!
Troy's walls blazed 'neath the lightning of thy eye!
Nymph of the bosom, from thy starlight brow
Millions have read their fate, even as I read it now.

XLVII.

The cataract, the wide fields, the rippling river,
The shubbery of green nature in its prime,
The warbling of the birds in summer weather,
The pleasing landscape glittering so sublime,
Are beautiful: but of the scenes of Time
Tall mountains are the grandest things I know;
And to their lofty region when I climb,
The awful tides of Feeling freer flow,
The big world circumscribing as they onward go.

XLVIII.

What would the haggard, war-ta'en captive give,
Who in the cold cell of some dungeon lies,
If, free, unshackled, here he could arrive,
If he could to these glorious summits rise:
When, mounted high, could with parental eyes
Behold his native home, and on its sward
His children sporting 'neath the daylight skies;
His wife submissive, toiling doubly hard
In his long absence; gaining with the industrious card,

XLXIX.

And spindle, something of a livelihood;
Indulging in God's mercy future hope,
That He will lift again the avenging rod,
And an unclouded azure once more ope?
His weary feelings would no longer droop;
But just imagine his triumphant state!
Woe's dreader chains, with which he had to cope,
Falling to earth, as now with joy await
His faithful dogs, to hail him at the wicket-gate.

L.

Down, down in the abyss of foaming ocean,
Tumbling in horrid hollows of the sea,
Wild rolled in the Atlantic's monstrous motion,
One waste of terrible eternity!
What would the storm-struck mariner give to be,
At such an hour, on these mild mountain tops?
Like me o'ercome with immortality;
Like me indulging in extensive hopes;
Like me observing starlight shores thro' sheeny loops!

LI.

Ye Titan-like vast Apennines! your bulk,
So beautifully huge, great things conceals.
Through your dark coverts midnight foxes sculk,
And many a mighty beast in terror steals.
And yet the cottager no horror feels:
There is a God who shuts the ravenous jaws;
To whom in evening prayer the peasant kneels,
And oft instructs his children in his laws:
"The watchman here wakes but in vain;" Heaven keeps his doors!

LII.

Have I not read thee, Southey, with delight;
And feasted upon Moore's bewitching lines?
Have I not wept on Burns who paints so bright
The love which our gross nature quite refines?
But Nature, with her elements, divines
The understanding far more than man's works;
When the huge lightning gilds the Apennines,
Then again mounting, in the tall cloud lurks,
And low beneath the thunderbolt's large shadow shirks

LIII.

'Twas here, oh! heavenizing be that thought!
The feet of our triumphant Scott once trode;
Tho' sickness, age, and toil had then near brought
This mighty genius, with their heavy load,
To his last home: that hour when griefs corrode
The bosom, and the frame not strong to bear.
Soon after, when o'er Scotia's deep he rode,
He viewed his Tweed once more, and then died there:
And yet these summits tower, though *such men* melt
in air.

LIV.

Here Passion pines for things it can't obtain;
The mind expatiates on great heroes' deeds;
Swelled with an impulse, longs in power to gain
Fame's loftiest peak; because it cannot—bleeds!
Tho' its aspiring thoughts must turn to weeds,
'Tis fearful when the enormous mind is bowed!
When all the grand ideas, on which it feeds,
Seem but a vain invention, an air cloud;
And weep upon its loss Ambition's strugglings loud!

LV.

When Gray, perched high on Snowdon's shaggy top,
Gave implements of vengeance to his bard;
While Edward, as 'twere deathstruck, could not cope,
With that high one whom heaven seem'd but to guard;
Oh, how the whole vast army shook and feared!
And dark Despair his huge sword seemed to unsheath;
When, ere the bard for ever disappeared,
His eye glanced wild in its last glance of death;
Thus springing from the dizzy peaks, he sank beneath!

LVI.

When Milton made a battle-plain of heaven,
And caused the two Archangels as dread foes
To meet; yes! when his powerful pen had given
The height of grandeur to the theme he chose;
A battailous great pageant then arose,
Volumes of brazen shields and massive spears,
The helmets which scowl fierce o'er angels' brows;
Outrageous batteries high tiers on tiers,
The tumbling down of burning stars and mighty spheres.

LVII.

These two are specimens of thought's extent;
And many more as splendid might be named;
Where Byron the huge Alps with terrors rent,
Or where old Rokeby's towers remorseless flamed.
How many a boy's attention is oft claimed
With these, when Shakspeare's grandeur gets too deep;
When the proud eminence, for which he aimed,
O'erlooks too terrible and vast a steep;
That youth's imagination cannot steady keep.

LVIII.

Yet to the question. Where, oh! where is he,
Whose supernatural energies of mind
Made him desert the Warwick swains to be
A listener of heaven? Yes! he could find,
In the strong hurricane and fearful wind,
In the inspiring elemental roll,
In the proud tempests of the o'erwhelming kind,
In making yon supernal realm his goal,
A stronger food to nourish his unbounded soul!

LXIX.

The inimitable Shakspeare! see him shining
'Mid the great thousand poets that have been,
Upon his brilliant throne in pomp reclining,
Just like the mighty moon within the sheen
Of million upon million stars! Serene
His eyes review them crouching at his feet;
The nine proud Muses smile on this vast scene;
The World a city, decked with many a street,
And fine inhabitants who now Fame's darling greet.

LX.

The fire of Milton was a dwindling flame
To the fine glory of that earth-spread blaze,
Characterizing the imperial fame
Of everlasting Shakspeare's grand displays
Of understanding's force; mere childish rays
To the omnipotence of his ideas.
He scorned even Jonson's fame in his best plays,
(The simile love, or love not, as ye please)
Just as the ocean whirlwind trifles with the breeze.

LXI.

His genius was unequalled; which could spurn
The dross of earth, above the clouds to soar;
Who caused, as 'twere, new luminaries to burn.
And made the big sky heaven's imperial floor;
Ocean with mightier mountain waves to tower;
Old Tartarus with kingly men to abound;
Lavished more sweet, and variegated, shower
Of beams upon the rainbow; and he wound
Around the earth for rural flowers a lovelier ground.

LXII.

Well I remember, when a little boy,
How I viewed Shakespeare's portrait with delight;
With a kind of enthusiastic joy,
As my fond parents told me of the might
Of his majestic powers—immortal quite.
They gazed so sweet upon me as I leant
With admiration o'er his features bright;
And well I recollect my mother bent
To print the mother's kiss, and then to tears gave vent.

LXIII.

To thee, illustrious Gregory,* adieu!
How fair a morning smiled upon thy birth!
Auspicious Prophecy a green wreath threw
Of laurels round thy infant brow of mirth.
Yet who could tell thus great would be thy worth?
Much the world saw in thy maturity;
For thy big genius lightened mother Earth;
And many a mazy labyrinth did espy
With the acute sagacity of Learning's eye.

LXIV.

When the nurse rocked the cradle for the child,
When the nurse humm'd the soothing lullaby,
And, looking on its innocent features, smiled,
Did she think of its future majesty?
Did she imagine that *wee* thing would be
One of the lords upon the illustrious side
Of Science; and that all the world should see
His banners floating, in their strength of pride,
Thro' Learning's pompous Capitol, for e'er to abide?

* This was written, and inserted here, when the sad tidings reached us of the death of the eminent Gregory.

LXV.

Hark! for the voice addresses our dull race;
It tells us what a champion we have lost;
It asks the question, "Who shall fill his place,
Of Cambridge' ancient towers the glorious boast?"
Yes! Death, the arch-monster, all his high schemes crossed;
He had not mounted to his loftiest point.
Still of his embers shall we make the most;
Oft shall the sorrowing tears our cheeks anoint,
But they shall leave behind a path of golden tint.

LXVI.

And thou art gone in manhood's prime away,
When near attaining Fame's meridian steep;
When all exulted at thy rising day,
Whose harvest many a student hoped to reap.
Ah! ever art thou gone—in vain we weep;
And low indeed that most majestic head
Dark Death has bent. Yet firm our love to keep,
We will plant flowers about thy last chill bed,
Even where great Gregory now slumbers with the dead.

LXVII.

Such able men as these more proudly move,
Their great shades flit more grandly thro' the brain,
When on tall mountain-tops we think so of
The unfathomable past; and that long chain
Of old events is pictured far more plain.
Deeds of whatever sort press with more force
On the ennobled soul; an endless train
Of sentimental thought here has its source,
Here unmolested may pursue its boundless course.

LXVIII.

Men of the highest stamp we muse upon,
Till, in a dream, we seem as one of them:
Imagination's lamp has full outshone,
And who the torrents of the heart can stem?
You must exert a power to quell the stream
In its first rising, ere it rush too strong;
And like Niagara's boiling cataracts steam,
Bearing all sober thoughts with it along,
Till it nears that dread pitch where wild floods ever throng;

LXIX.

And burst their way through precipices thrown
By the convulsive effort round rough shores;
Reeling like tumbling thunder-bolts adown
The rugged pits where Desolation roars:
From whose dark cave the eagle never soars;
Where the despairing Indian only throws
Himself in passion's ignorance; nor to pause
Stays; but from the whirlpool of Time's woes,
Hoping his case to improve, unto a worse fate goes.

LXX.

But in this strain a book I could dictate;
Yet what is said suffices. And once more,
Nor yet too frequent, view the regal state
Of the fine Apennines still o'er and o'er.
Wonder, feel dignified, you must adore;
Sublimity, whate'er ye want, here is;
Let your souls leap, and let your visions tower,
Yes! tower on wings of glory through the abyss,
Where, as ye gaily soar, there'll meet you stars of bliss.

LXXI.

Gew-gaws appear to gild Italia's woods,
For yon orbs' golden showers pour such a gleam,
That brilliancy from every tree exudes,
Or seems to exude;—a marvellous rich dream.
What can contend with the refulgent beam
That shines so fair from sun and stars and moon?
The chandeliers of emperors, that stream
In grand show down the imperial saloon?
Put them in that 'mid arch! the question's answer'd soon.

LXXII.

On high, on high! just fix them in yon heaven,
In that big world of proud magnificence!
And then observe how swift they would be given
To Lethe's endless sea. Such empty nonsense
In every honour where man makes pretence
Of grandeur. For such things light some small room;
But in the terrible circumference
Of Nature, drown they scarce one inch of gloom;
Like some vain Jack-o'-lantern, shortly meet their doom.

LXXIII.

Ye starry gems! which streak the purple air,
And gild for angels pathways through the skies;
Ye wonders so unutterably fair,
Ye orbs which darken Argus' hundred eyes!
How soft ye gleam where sleeping India lies!
Oft when a child regarding you, I thought
The wild outlaw considers you a prize,
As from his dun cave he views heaven in-wrought
With tissue of most sparkling gold, rays from ye caught.

LXXIV.

Balls of a size immense we cannot measure,
Though mortals' dim eyes see but twinkling specks;
Even small as spangling gold-dust, such a treasure
To divers in the east, who near the wrecks
Of mighty ships sink down; and each one seeks
Pearls, blazing diamonds, rubies, amethysts:
As small as these ye seem, more pure your streaks;
To hear if music dwell in you one lists;
For who, and what ye are, my vision never wists.

LXXV.

I gaze on yon calm heaven—yon placid stars,
And then reflect what contrast they present
To the world's nations, their intestine wars,
To the vain hate to which they give such vent:
Thus fond affection is in pieces rent,
And man destroys the green vales of sweet Bliss.
Benignant stars! that, on your courses bent,
Glance at each other with such hues of peace,
And hand in hand roam through Eternity's abyss.

LXXVI.

Review the suicide weltering in his blood,
The tool of Vice in its degraded form;
Dark leaping from his veins the headlong flood,
Horrible to be seen—with life yet warm!
Then, having thus beheld so fierce a storm
Of man's atrocious passion, look at heaven;
Its matchless features, its young eyes, which swarm
Like isles of light upon ye; yonder seven
Young Pleiades, the milky ways to cheer you given.

LXXVII.

How glorious do the crystal hills surround
The clear waves of the Caspian, as they roll
Over that beautiful enchanted ground,
That he who gazes on it feels his soul
Rise very mightily. So on this mole
Of Time, I see around the ethereal main,
High towering and o'er-beetling each far pole,
More precious mountains wrought of gold-dust, ta'en
From unseen shores, which thrill me with triumphant strain.

LXXVIII.

Oh, what a lovely treat a bright star is!
How sweet to see the fair moon by its side!
When Night affords you an o'erwhelming bliss,
Bathed brilliantly in splendour's silvery tide!
Ah! could I but upon its large orbs ride,
And feel their rampant frenzy fire me through;
No more I would on this vile earth abide,
But choose the proud empyrean in lieu;
Yet still your towers, O Apennines, should cheer my view.

LXXIX.

It is most exquisite to look at heaven,
Even when hooded o'er with heavy clouds:
Majestic prospects to the eye are given,
As the tremendous conflagration broods.
But tear away for me these pompous shrouds,
And ope the blue, display the starlight calm;
Within yon shining sea let there be crowds
Of spangling planets, like a glittering swarm
Of bright-eyed cherubs breathing everlasting balm.

LXXX.

Imagination! take thy mightiest stretch—
Fancy! thy royal walking-ground behold!
Man! actest thou not like a bestial wretch,
Even to forego the blaze of fields of gold,
Of Heaven's profoundest imagery unrolled,
Of stars, like palaces of Paradise,
Of planets whose rich dalliance ne'er was told,
Of all those exquisitely-twinkling eyes,
For the vile wallowing in night's debaucheries?

LXXXI.

On this huge mountain could I lie and sleep;
The great moon for my lantern, and the stars
My guardian angels. Lost in yon far deep,
Whose surface is so tinged with gorgeous spars,
Thus sink in slumber's arms, thus drown the cares,
Which, if we should not have, we ourselves make;
Thus stranger, for a time, to mental wars,
Till the gay gleams of morning on us break,
And wildly-bounding animals tell all to awake.

LXXXII.

But, O my spirit, let us scorn the idea!
Sleep I forsake this night to contemplate.
The stars shall burn quite out, and likewise she,
The high, fair moon, ere my mind take its bait.
With joyful patience shall my soul await
To see Aurora, like an empress, shine;
Driving in costly chariot of state,
Drawn by gold-harnessed steeds, and dressed out fine,
Horsed cherubs riding, by her car, with power divine.

LXXXIII.

On mountain terraces when calm reclining,
Oft muse I on Geneva's moon-lit lake;
Weeping abundant floods of tears, and pining
Invoke Tell's noble ashes to awake.
I prize those famed scenes for their hero's sake.
Oh! in my school-days what exulting joy
Burst from each sense, when, his son's life at stake,
The arrow, aimed with judgment, cast the die,
Struck off the apple. How I loved this when a boy!

LXXXIV.

Welcome to me, ye masters of the earth!
Bright as the gorgeous latitude of heaven,
Do you, the children of immortal birth,
Blaze to my admiration! ye are given
Earth, ocean, ocean's islands, to enliven;
Grand stars of great Creation's lower state!
Paragons of mankind! Like Græcia's seven
Wise ones, ye walk the world with emperor-gait;
And scorn the frowns of Envy, Pride, and rancorous Hate!

LXXXV.

My mind gets whelmed, at such a shining spring
Of glories drinking; and my vision reels,
Which just now floated on a wavy wing,
To earth quite surfeited; and through me steals
A flood of raptures, that each new thought swells,
Quite undistinguishable, their power so vast;
And Passion opes her hundred-gated cells,
To feast her appetite on such repast.
Yet shall I rise again, nor deign to be o'ercast!

LXXXVI.

It seems as if a most ambrosial throng
Of fairies gave my mouth from glittering cups
The juicy nectar. For here sweeps along
A glancing foot; and here a white breast opes
To view; and here through pale and ivory loops
A dark eye flashes with luxurious wile;
In elegant fatigue a swan-neck droops,
And young lips shew the white teeth as they smile;
And here a sweet form languishes—but not from toil.

LXXXVII.

My mind, in an unutterable frame
For musing, mounts on pinions madly strong;
Heaven's beauteous, broad display of starlight flame,
Scenes that I can't describe bear it along!
Forgive me that thus lowly is the song,
When in a world so fitting to inspire;
For white-robed cherubims in cycles throng
The distant isles of gold,—and while the fire
Of transport thrills me much, I even hear their lyre.

LXXXVIII.

'Tis the eternal hymn they seem to sing,
Which floats triumphant through the rushing air!
Behold the flash of many a golden wing,
The rosy cheek of many a cherub fair.
No harmony of man can we compare
With this—ah me! his richest strains are weak:
When even hundreds in grand chorus share,
And make earth's kings with admiration quake!
One angel's voice can louder, sweeter music make;

"Hallelujah, hallelujah!"
Sounds from harps of gold high strung;
"Hallellujah, hallellujah!"
Bursts from every seraph's tongue.

Am I now in heaven or not?
Cherubs, solve the mystery!
Am I now in heaven or not,
Where the happy valleys lie?

Perfumed roses wreath these islets—
Surely I cannot be dreaming;
Perfumed roses wreath these islets,
Smiles upon blue seas are gleaming.

Palms of green are glittering here,
Angels bind them round their brows;
Palms of green are glittering here,
Near where ocean ever flows.

Surely I must be in heaven,
This can never be a cheat!
Surely I must be in heaven,
Earth has no abode so sweet!

"Hallelujah, hallelujah!"
Sounds from harps of gold high strung;
"Hallelujah, hallelujah!"
Bursts from every seraph's tongue!

LXXXIX.

Ye Apennines! when first I climbed your peaks,
I hinted that in joys I might forget
Myself ofttimes: 'tis time my mind now takes
A train of thought more sober, to correct
These rushing tides; or Fancy soon may get
The mastery over me her rightful lord.
O Fancy! thy best dreams so shortly set!
Their shining lips but speak an empty word;
The light hands of their spirits no true aid afford!

XC.

In times of old, when pirates swarmed the seas,
And the scull-flag forebode man's destiny,
Flapping, like Death, amid the doleful breeze,
The sign that hurled him to Eternity.
At such a period one could never be
Safe when he sailed to India's pearl-zoned isles;
And social sailors shuddered then to see
The bark in the horizon with white sails:
Now almost wholly rid of these, how ocean smiles!

XCI.

Time was when, 'mid these half impervious passes,
Tribes of banditti hid their dangerous spoils:
Behold among those huge gigantic masses,
May be, what are the relics of their toils.
Caves, subterraneous caves, where one recoils—
Starts back with horror! once their dim abodes:
Here round the fire raged their intestine broils;
Where they displayed, each man, the glittering loads
Of silver or of gold, o'er which the mind corrodes.

XCII.

And these have passed—their hour was very brief,
The cowl you now behold through midnight's phases;
At least seen outwardly, the robber chief,
Who scaled rude rocks, whose course no step retraces,
Who loved to brood in dark, wild, dismal places,
Contrasted with the monkish look of these,
The solemn cast of their religious faces,
Seems the fierce monster; for we ever please
To judge by outward aspects, and the formal knees.

XCIII.

The judgment, truly terrible, will shew
That oft "the first are last, the last are first."
Behold the wretched dying thief! and lo!
He now forgets his agony, his worst
Of torture, as grand Feeling seems to outburst
With voice sublime on top of Calvary,
In arms of Faith triumphant gladly nursed,
"Lord! in thy kingdom pray remember me!"
Oh, pitch in truth of most exulting ecstacy!

XCIV.

Newton's proud telescope ne'er saw that God,
Who wheels his chariot o'er the hills of clouds;
Who down the howling whirlwind paves a road,
Embosomed in the rattling tempest's shrouds.
Here in his suite are the angelic crowds;
Heaven's high Archangel for his charioteer;
The globe his footstool, where his ire oft broods;
Above the sky his gorgeous thrones appear;—
Canst thou, great Being! condescend to view man's
sphere?

XCV.

But Feeling's ebullition stays not here;
It has a loftier goal to which to carry
Its big intents, and where it will uprear
Huger designs, and never more be weary:
Where o'er sublimer scenery it shall tarry,
Extravagantly robed in grandeur's dress;
Where o'er that blue expanse, so cool, so airy,
Wax beautiful the fields of pleasantness,
Glittering with lovely sights which Heaven e'er deigns to bless.

XCVI.

And this is but the embryo beginning
Of that which shall be far more mighty soon;
The Soul I mean, which ever will be winning
Our hearts to regions past yon gentle moon,
Whose brilliant days can never see a noon:
There shall our low conceptions be exchanged
For understandings which will make us swoon
At first on shores of rapture, where ne'er clanged
Man's foot; for in such mansions he would feel deranged.

XCVII.

Exult—rejoice! oh, dash to earth the tear!
In this clay cell thy bondage is not long,
Mysterious Soul. Thy bearers shall appear,
Unsullied seraphims, a startling throng,
And then—yes! then shalt thou sing Victory's song!
Meanwhile I counsel thee, "Do not despair;
Let patience' calm thy features roam among;
Indulge not in the unmeaning fretful stare,
Which mars thy loveliness, and makes thee seem less fair."

XCVIII.

One early recollection, printed deep,
Deep in the memory, I must mention now;
Whose scenes of mournful grandeur sadly creep
Within the bosom, solemnly and slow;
Much heightened on these Apennines' wild brow!
They are of one who died when she was young,
And beautiful; whose turn of mind, I trow,
Was too refined and gentle to belong
To the world's noisy denizens—that barbarous throng!

XCIX.

In boyhood an Italian once I met;
I first passed by; but seeing an eye so sad,
His long dark lashes too with grief's showers wet,
It made me halt. The noble mien he had
Was much bedimmed by Sorrow's gloomy shade.
To look, was to admire his handsome face,
Which seemed as if 'twould never more beam glad.
He beckoned me to sit down on a place
Contiguous to all pleasures, that one loves to trace.

C.

From where we sate the view was beautiful:
A town on one side, on the other smiled
A most luxurious river. Near, the school
Of my glad childhood was: its walls high piled;
Its stately portico our sight beguiled;
The playground reached even to this river's bank:
My merry schoolmates' echoes our hearts thrilled;
It was a pleasant sound, which leaves a blank
In after days, when one thinks how he deeply drank

CI.

From Joy's wild-flowing stream in childhood's hours.
And the Italian in appearance seemed
To feel the same; for faster now the showers
Of unfeigned agony from his eyes streamed—
Such fleeting pleasures, one seems to have dreamed!
Moreover little children told their tales
One to another; here some loudly screamed;
Here some were sporting with rude-bounding balls;
Some with long staffs moved boats decked out with paper sails.

CII.

The very spot for a romantic taste;
To cause a lover sentimental sorrow.
The sunlight beamed most exquisitely chaste
On the smooth river's breast and banks; while thro'
The limpid waves ye saw the young fish glow,
Flash back again from golden-tinted scales
The rays of heaven. As white as starlight snow
Reclining in the breast of gelid dales,
The water-lilies shone, protected from fierce gales.

CIII.

What made the whole more beautiful, more sweet,
Even was the silvery sound of far church-bells,
Echoing so placid through the aerial sheet,
Winding through valleys, and luxuriant dells.
To catch that sound, oh! how the bosom swells,
And how it thrills with ecstacy the frame!
Awaking us, just like the voice which tells
Us we are loved by one alone the same,
That being which ever bears a magic in her name.

CIV.

I own the howling tempest comes with grandeur,
When clouds, like towering citadels, adown
The vault of sky descend on dreadful tour,
And wrap all heaven and earth in solemn frown.
When the wild ocean wears a tinge of brown,
Caught from the frightened sun's strange peeping eye
Through darkness bursting; and dark thunders blown
On whirlwinds' madness little man defy,
As he stands trembling at the torn and shattered sky.

CV.

The momentary inspiration caught
From such fierce warfare never truly lasts;
First, lightning-like, the flashing of swift thought
Ascends, but is put out by quenching blasts;
And, as a dying rainbow, dimly casts
Its shadow o'er the splendour of the heaven.
'Tis on a *quiet* spot that feeling feasts,
Where thousand beauties to the eye are given,
Magnificently tender, heart and soul to enliven.

CVI.

Such was this scene. And soon the Italian broke
The silence that had reigned 'tween us sometime.
Of Italy's great lords he freely spoke,
Of famed Lorenzo, of Berni sublime,
Of Dante's powers, of Catalani's chime.
And then he sadly smiled, and in strange ways
Spake wildly; while I stedfast gazed on him;
At last his fine eye quivered with a blaze;
Then told he me this doleful tale of other days.

CVII.

"The faith of her forefathers did she change,
She took the veil, thenceforth became a nun;
Yes, she! with whom in youth I used to range,
Whom I loved as a boy. I felt undone!
The fairy being of my childhood won
In such a way for ever from my arms.
Yes! when her life of solitude begun,
I mourned her inexpressible, young charms:
She's now in isles of peace where nothing her soul harms.

CVIII.

"There is a convent in a lovely isle,
(Hilda, for secrecy, shall be its name);
Emerging from green vales its turrets smile,
And oft the attention of the pilgrim claim.
The scene by sea and land would beat the aim
Of any artist, its fair mien to paint.
'Twas here the exquisite Theresa came,
With this world's heavy cares oppressed, and faint,
To pass her transient term of days—to die a saint.

CIX.

"The deep blue of the ocean brightly ran
Along the outskirts of calm Hilda's bounds,
Which many a radiant rainbow loved to span
After a day of tempest's thundering sounds;
Like those rich lights upon the Enchanted grounds.
St. Hilda too shone well with fruitful trees,
With palms that glittered on grass-studded mounds,
With cypresses that waved beneath the breeze,
With graceful weeping willows, her young nuns to please.

CX.

" And wide indeed was Hilda's fair domain,
No cost was spared to deck it with fine groves:
Here was the open undulating plain,
Here the recess where one more secret roves;
Here were the pastures for the lowing droves;
And here all day would frisk the bleating sheep:
Such a scene altogether one so loves!
A scene quite blended both of land and deep,
Which melts the heart so much, emotion makes it weep.

CXI.

" Beautiful shone the valley where did lie,
As if in marble sleep, old Hilda's towers;
From a high slope of hills, one could espy
Their splendid turrets gilt with sunbeam's showers.
A pious baron, in his dying hours,
Bequeathed unto the church these noble halls:
Here Beauty, having built her sweetest bowers,
And girded it around with lovely walls,
To many a nun from far, with invitation calls.

CXII.

" Oaks that a thousand years had bravely stood
The violent tempest, the fierce hurricane,
The horrid hailstorm's desolating flood,
Smiled green on many an undulating plain.
From their broad branches, in the evening's wane,
The summer cuckoo's note in gladness rose:
Pet deer there lay in hours of heat and rain
Beneath their shades; and after daylight's close
The nightingale by moonlight sang upon their boughs.

CXIII.

"Here gaily crowed the cock at blink of dawn;
And sky-larks breathed their whelming melody;
Soaring to heaven from many a sloping lawn,
Mid the far blue fields of eternity.
Here flowery hedges blooming might you see,
And hear the small birds twittering 'mong their leaves;
Sometimes they hopped about from tree to tree;
Sometimes they thronged the banks where Phœbus weaves
A serpentine gold path, as Hilda's river heaves.

CXIV.

"For you must know a cooling river wound
About old Hilda's beautiful domain;
And girded its unmatched estates around,
Just like a silvery serpent on a plain.
At last its waters met the purple main.
Where these united towered to heaven a crag,
On which the ruins of an olden fane;
But now it formed a battery with a flag,
And near it gleamed a lighthouse hoary with its age.

CXV.

"Two precipices frown'd with giant steeps,
Round which the rattling surges rudely splashed;
And towered oft, vast as icebergs, heaps on heaps!
Then thunder-like against the big rocks crashed.
They say in storms 'twas fearful; for they lashed
These cloud-capped precipices till they shook;
Their spray against the lighthouse' summits dashed.
One awful boisterous night a whirlwind took
This chapel's roof into the sea, and its walls broke.

CXVI.

"Upon a howling night had ye been there,
You might have deemed that Pharaoh's host was dying;
Such startling noises rolled along the air,
Such frantic sea-fowl ominously crying,
And down the abyss, from billows madly flying,
One might have thought, each lightning flake he saw,
Chariots were foundering, and their proud steeds lying
Gasping in anguish on the roaring shore;
So dread a conflagration one ne'er viewed before.

CXVII.

"Ne foreign people trespassed on these peaks;
Ne men indeed of worldly character.
But monks themselves, who risked their own dear sakes
For other folk, here stationed ever were.
On many a sea-girt rock their minds would rear
Temples of fancy, where they might devote
To their Creator, every thought and fear;
Where over the abyss they might be brought
To admiration, courting Neptune's lordly note!

CXVIII.

"And till this river blended with the ocean,
Through many a pleasant scene it wound its way.
The weeping willows, waving in sweet motion,
Studding its sides in exquisite array,
And other trees, too numerous to say,
Shaded its verdant ever-lilied banks.
Moreover all throughout the night and day,
Both black and snow-white swans, in graceful ranks,
Sailed its clear bosom yielding their Creator thanks.

CXIX.

"And where the river and the ocean met,
On the tall crags Theresa ofttimes sate,
Viewing the blood-red sun in grandeur set;
A sight than which none ever was more great.
Here would she muse upon our mortal fate;
And not unfrequent might ye hear her sigh:
She thought on Eve's and Adam's lost estate,
And how they piled a mass of misery,
Immeasurable, for their forlorn posterity.

CXX.

"The long, high rolling of the ocean tides,
The mountain billows bellowing in their course,
The fine commanding view where each crag strides,
The maddened sea-gulls shrieking themselves hoarse,
Made it of wild romance the grandest source;
For, oh! 'twas splendid on a glorious day!
Here undisturbed each nun had free recourse
To meditation dignified; to pray,
Or read, or think, came here quite natural in their way.

CXXI.

"To strangers Hilda's portals were e'er shut,
Thus the serene that reigned was very sweet;
The groves round were comparatively mute,
Save the birds' songs, or sounds of fairy feet,
In green recesses where nuns loved to meet.
'Twas scarcely self denial living thus:
But here Retirement could afford a treat,
A place where her devoted ones might muse
Better than in life's gayer scenes; and this its use.

CXXII.

"But such joys to Theresa were not long.
Those skies that lit, those seas that girt, that isle,
Her dear companions, that delightful throng!
Were enjoyed by her but a transient while.
Whether from illness, or ascetic toil,
Her frail frame daily seemed to fast decay;
And many an one with anguish saw her smile
Wax fainter gradually day by day;
Till at last, like a rainbow, passed that smile away.

CXXIII.

"The closing, solemn hours of her short life,
Pillowed upon her couch, she loved to see
The sky above without one cloud of strife,
Beneath it beaming Hilda's ocean sea.
She saw thy gloriousness, Eternity,
Pictured within the mighty frame of each.
And oft she started at the well-known cry,
As she surveyed the calm and sleeping beach,
When floated loud through realms of air the sea-gull's
screech.

CXXIV.

"Oh! 'twas most piteous, past description's power,
To see Theresa lingering in that state;
For the last time on many a favourite bower,
Or on some pet lamb which appeared to await
Her deathly-eye now looking, spite of Fate.
There was a piercing gleam in her last gaze!
Which, as her hour of life was waxing late,
Burned still more radiant in the wane of days,
And moons, which lit St. Hilda with their tearful rays.

CXXV.

"If she had any thing to leave behind,
Or any pleasures here for which she cared,
Such humble things were they which would scarce bind
Another mortal to that earth prepared
She was to leave. And though she well had shared
Her deep affection with each sister nun;
Yet, when the final summons now appeared,
Submissively to One as she begun
Her course, she felt submissive now to that great One.

CXXVI.

"The last, sad evening that she spent on earth,
Shone beautiful around the radiant shores
Of Hilda's isle; as when the famous birth
Of Cytheræa caused the purple doors
Of ocean to emerge; the rough sea's roars
Were ceased; yet rustling breezes heaved a groan.
Such was that noonday, over which deplores
Many a young heart in green bowers alone;
Those thoughts which cause the monarch tears upon his throne.

CXXVII.

"No brighter day o'er Hilda's island gleamed
Than that one which saw fair Theresa die:
They who beheld her end thought that they dreamed,
So still her spirit passed, without a sigh.
A sunbeam lit the chamber radiantly,
And sweetly hovered round her pallid charms;
Like some immortal chariot passing by,
To bear her o'er the din of time's alarms,
Unto a more enduring rest, 'mid endless calms.

CXXVIII.

" Thus died Theresa. And that morn she breathed
Her last, my bark did hail the sorrowing beach;
Where Hilda, by Aurora's chaplet wreathed,
Lay in its beauty. Nought but some wild screech,
Which seemed desirous by sad sounds to teach
Me of Theresa's fate, I first could hear;
The sailors whispered calmly each to each;
Their uncouth, yet real, sympathy did appear
Most pleasing, as they saw me drop the noiseless tear.

CXXIX.

" We had now neared the fair, yet mournful, shore;
When, through the breeze, the solemn-sounding bell
Tolled for that one we never should see more,
So truly melancholy in its knell!
Ne'er a more gloomy story could it tell.
No stranger, as I said before, could land
On this part of the island; for so well,
And strictly, kept the convent's solemn band;
Such order caused their piety to shine more grand.

CXXX.

" Therefore we kept our bark some distance out;
But still St. Hilda's turrets beamed in view:
And till her funeral day I sate quite mute,
And stared quite vacantly upon the blue
Of ocean. When the fourth day shone anew,
Upon its noon again the funeral note
Of Hilda in its island breezes blew
Within my ear, and on my bosom smote;
I stood upon the deck, and these few lines I wrote:—

"The bell tolled loud in Hilda's tower,
The convent dirge rose sweet, yet sad;
The noonday burst in pompous power,
The skies scarce any dimness had.

"On the blue of the liquid sea
A pinnace came there softly stealing;
An angel of eternity,
One might have thought, its white wings swelling.

"It stayed close by the sacred shore,
Where Hilda's solemn turrets are;
And landed nuns, in number four,
Of islet regions from afar.

"At such a beauteous, yet sad, time,
The charms of woman dart more bright;
They passed us by—their looks sublime
Seemed gilted with a saintly light!

"Though pale with sorrow their young cheeks,
Religion loved their minds to teach;
For Peace hued, with angelic streaks,
The splendid countenance of each.

"At their arrival deeper tolled
The swinging bell with gloomier sounds;
That bell so many years now old,
Which hallowed Hilda's sacred grounds!

"Beautiful was that noon I said;
The sea-breeze fanned the rosy hills;
The glittering ocean lustre shed,
The wild birds shrieked through joyous bills.

"No mountain wave tremendous rose,
No breaker rolled along the coast;
But all was calm—all was repose—
On the deep slept the sunny host.

"If a cloud rose upon the eye,
It was a cloud most richly bright;
Those clouds that so improve the sky,
Commingling with its golden light.

"'Twas one of those impressive eves,
Whose radiance monarchs in the skies,
Telling, in each sweet ray it weaves,
Beyond the West's far gate heaven lies.

"But many a gentle breast was aching,
And many an eye was wet with tears!
Ah! many a woman's heart was breaking,
And many a soul was filled with fears.

"For as a beaming flower full blown,
Just in the bloom of loveliest pride,
Theresa laid her meekly down,
Drooping awhile, serenely died.

" This being was fairest of the fair
Of all in Hilda's holy sphere;
And none that ever entered there,
Had powerful beauty, like to her.

" Of blue, such as Australia's sky,
Were her unutterable orbs;
That hue which, even in mildest dye,
All other earthly hues absorbs.

" On her commanding open brow
A light shone, like a star sublime,
That one up-gazing from below
Sees in the spangled roof of time.

" In golden showers long auburn hair,
At the meridian of her day,
Swept down Theresa's shoulders fair,
In exquisitely grand array.

" Its glittering clusters, when unrolled,
Would even touch her tapery feet;
My boyhood read in tales of old
Of fairies' charms that were less sweet.

" But soon as she became a nun,
That floating hair was cast away;
Her loveliness, when this was done,
Was not obscured by plain array.

"Her stature elegantly grand,
Majestic her most careless mien:
Fair rose she in the glistening band,
As if she mortal had not been.

"The pensive look she often had,
More beautified her piercing eye;
And shed a kind of placid shade,
But far was it from melancholy.

"Have your eyes ever chanced to fall
Upon some condor on a rock,
Listening to heaven's loud thunder-ball,
And hearing earth groan 'neath the shock?

"Then see the lightning leave his eyes,
And grandly tower his august form;
So fine!—he fills you with surprise,
A splendid thing amid the storm!

"Nobler the aspect of this one,
On whom *too many a storm* had spent
Its rage in vain, and fallen down
Quite vanquished from its element.

"Oh! say not this is fancy's way,
To rate a woman's charms too high;
No force on earth can stronger sway
The mind than maiden majesty!

"For such an one the funeral bell
Was tolling now through Hilda's tower;
What pen describe, or what tongue tell,
The feeling of that solemn hour?

"But Death, on his mighty palace dome,
When he sweeps away the film of clouds,
And sees through the blue skies her pale tomb,
Shall mantle himself in mourning shrouds!

"Hark! for a ding dong bursts the smooth air,
Not in chariot of thunders floats its strain!
But the zephyr's light wings its notes bear,
Along the aerial azure plain.

"Stretched was her coffin on that bed,
Where sweet in life-time she had slept;
You could not hear one single tread,
A horror o'er the assembly crept!

"The Abbess raised the coffin lid,
And ne'er outburst a lovelier sight!
There lay Theresa as she died,
Calm sleeping, like an angel bright.

"Immensely grand is it to view
The angelic softness of the dead;
For the sprite does not bid adieu,
But still loves there pale light to shed.

"You almost in a dream can trace
Its newly lit, and heavenized ray;
Hovering around the placid face,
Exulting over dark Decay.

"They sleep so calm, they lie so still,
We often long, like them, to be;
They seem so loving to God's will,
So much resigned; and thus was she.

"White as a sheet her listless form,
No breath, no groan, no heaving sigh;
The stillness that succeeds the storm—
One cannot deem it apathy!

"More captivating than in life—
Ah! one's dear friends are little known,
Are slightly prized, until the strife
Of the last struggle e'er has flown!

"Then as upon the corpse we gaze
Affection takes its root so deep;
We muse on faded moons, and days,
And lift our voices up, and weep.

"We think of all the griefs we cost
The one that now so helpless lies;
Of opportunities e'er lost
To offer sorrow's sacrifice.

"And when the mild forgiving look
From the belovèd corpse appears
To shine, oh! who *that look* can brook?
Oh! who can stop the bursting tears?

"Her fingers, pale as gelid snow,
Were crossed upon her silent breast;
While her calm aspect seemed to shew
How blissful is the saint's last rest!

"Her silver-lidded eye, half closed,
Allowed one blue gleam to dart forth,
To say how sweetly she reposed
After the evening of Death's wrath.

"On her young bosom, more than fair,
The crucifix, she oft had pressed
Unto her lips, lay glimmering there,
For this her dying, last, request.

"The Abbess gazed, then her eyes she raised,
And seemed to breathe a silent prayer;
And the nuns did chime their funeral hymn,
With a sad and melancholy air!

"But the bell so old now heavier tolled,
And the last fond look must soon be o'er;
Oh! so gloomy the sound now rolled around,
That it pierced to every bosom's core!

"'Peace with her ashes be,' now said
The Abbess, as she closed the lid;
'Never a purer spirit fled,
Never one more triumphant died!'

"Oh! hear them go, with solemn steps of woe,
The nuns and Abbess to the grave;
There's not one eye in the assembly dry;
And dolefully the kerchiefs wave.

"Now a silence reigns, like that in the plains
Of heaven, upon a murky night;
As when we tread o'er the mounds of the dead,
And shudder even as our footsteps light!

"Thus they halt round her cold tomb,
While the priest slow reads the prayers;
And his low voice sounds full of gloom,
And glides o'er aisles and winding stairs.

"Now the sound ding dong no more rolls along,
For the chapel bell has ceased to toll;
And in chambers deep the nuns now weep,
Praying for fair Theresa's soul!

"See! yonder sleeps her blessed shade,
'Neath arches towering lies her tomb;
Her soul shall shed, which ne'er can fade,
Eternal light around that gloom.

"When dying Phœbus smiled no more,
When twilight's rosy beams had set;
As the moon rose on Hilda's shore,
Its look I never shall forget:

"For it was weeping silvery tears,
Which seemed to say, bedewing the sea,
'Past, past, are all your hopes and fears,
Theresa's in eternity!'

CXXXI.

"O early recollections, how ye fled!
Well I remember her sweet face in youth;
Her radiant eye, her auburn hair which shed
Such glory—charms that ripened with her growth.
The bright smile on her lips! in very truth
The holiest, the serenest I e'er saw—
Her elegance of stature; even forsooth
The more you gazed on, still ye loved it more:
The floating curls that angelized her neck's white shore.

CXXXII.

"Ah! Hilda's holy isle no more shall view
This flower of beauty in her sea-girt land;
Eclipsed for ever her fine eye of blue,
For ever deadened lies her snowy hand;
Which many a boon of charity made grand.
Yet the poor shall lament Theresa's fate;
And every Sabbath shall they sadly stand
By Hilda's gates to mourn her fallen state,
And ruminate in anguish, till eve grows quite late.

CXXXIII.

"Thus comes the iron tyranny of Fate;
Who deems it beautiful to see us wring
Our hands in agony, and then to hate
The unforgotten hour which did first bring
A being in the world to endure the sting,
The horrid lash of horrible Despair!
Why did a mother at our cradle sing
Her lullaby of joy, if after—care?
Didst Thou ordain this, God! didst Thou this woe prepare?"

CXXXIV.

I stopped him here; for floods of tears began
To dew his manly face; gigantic throes
Of grief made his breast heave; so pale, so wan,
He seemed half petrified; around his brows
The blue veins swelled; and now began to close
His faint, fair eyelids—thus he shortly drooped.
But all at once in madness he arose!
Then, as if some far beam of glory oped,
He looked at heaven quite wild, and seemed as if he hoped

CXXXV.

Theresa's angel form might now appear:
But when it did not, then he tore his hair,
And beat his brow; a pale and ashy fear
Sate on his lips; and on his breast so bare
He cut deep gashes; while an iron care
Frowned in his handsome yet distorted face.
As to the other horrors, I would spare
The feelings of the reader; nor would trace
The dreadful end of blasted love to its last place.

CXXXVI.

But I must cease to write in such sad strain,
And strive my page with rainbows to relieve:
But since, high-arched upon the ethereal plain,
They do not now their steps of radiance leave;
Come forth, fair flower, that I may cease to grieve;
"My kingdom" only for a small Heart's-ease!
Nature, upon these Apennines now weave
The colours of this flower my soul to please;
For woe's fierce-visaged phantoms e'er will my mind teaze.

CXXXVII.

Delightful germ! so striped with luscious hues,
Denominated long the sweet "Heart's-ease;"
Characteristic lineaments infuse
Themselves in thee, as even the child to please.
My aching breast would gladly take a lease,
And make thy petals its own lodging-place;
Even here each morn and e'en would bend its knees
To Nature's God, away all anguish chace;
Till life's quick-flowing sand hath run its fleeting race.

CXXXVIII.

My heart is vanquished, and the feelings melt;
Oh! what are like the throbs of wild delight!
Now beams faint o'er the eye Orion's belt,
Of starlike workmanship so purely bright;
And all those million blazing orbs of light
Have sunk quite suddenly, as if a sea,
Heaving with billows of enormous might,
Dashed against every twinkling luminary,
And quenched the lustre of the broidered galaxy.

CXXXIX.

The silver-pillow'd moon is sailing still;
But o'er the Apennines' far-stretching peaks,
A sunrise' tinge, that might an idiot thrill!
Gilds the horizon with vermilion streaks.
What startling radiance on the eyesight breaks!
The huntsman's restless dog begins to bark,
As he beholds the newly glittering lakes;
The grateful mountaineer is up; and hark!
The woodman's hatchet sounds, at daylight's early spark.

CXL.

Yet still regard the starless arch. What gleams
Thy panting hosts, O Morning, now present:
Rich bursts of fiery crimson, living streams
Of molten glory yon sky circumvent!
With flaming frenzy, on her day-course bent,
Glowing so healthy, and with cheeks so fair,
Aurora blows her trump—the skies are rent!
Here issuing orders from the royal chair,
Her chariot rattles loud thro' heaven's imperial air!

CXLI.

Had I the master pen of mighty Pope,
Or Thomson's matchless picturer of the scenes
Of Nature; even then the attempt must droop,
To pencil to the world what intervenes
These Apennines and heaven. Alas! what screens
Such noble pageant but the untutored vision?
Oh! how the sun each mountain-summit sheens!
Phaeton's steeds, rejoicing in their mission,
Prance on the crimson clouds and eye earth with derision.

CXLII.

How tame indeed, how brute-like are those souls
Which start not when they Morning's suite behold;
As through his burnished arch of splendour rolls
The King of day, who strides o'er heaven so bold!
The darkest gulleys drink his springs of gold
Which issue from an ever-trickling fount:
See! his most gorgeous drapery not worn old;
Though hoary Time sits care-worn on his mount
Of years six-thousand, and his days begins to count.

CXLIII.

Had not famed Dante dreams of Paradise,
Which he so ably pictured on his page?
Let him come forth! and yet, however wise,
Yon battlements of fire, in sparkling rage,
Shall try the proud description of that sage.
Mountains of gilt piled nobly 'thwart the sky;
More grand the well-experienced eye of age,
Though it had near roamed earth's rotundity,
Ne'er saw. They look on me with supercilious eye;

CXLIV.

E'en just as if I were some grovelling worm,
Lost in their blazing majesty of size!
Creeping in wonder, for life's transient term,
Beneath their bases broidered with gay dyes.
The eagle staggers near the sun, nor flies
So high as these enkindled piles to meet;
Their gaudy palace-halls no silver buys.
All we can do is, in the ethereal sheet
To enviously admire what flames so fine, yet sweet.

CXLV.

But time is sweeping on, or else my pen
Would portrait all that heaven and earth surrounds;
Would now desire to dwell upon and glean
From the birds' sonnets in these towering grounds
More joy than from that which the soul astounds,
When hundreds singing Handel whelm the world,
Shaking Great Britain's halls with godlike sounds!
Each note so pompous seeming wide unfurled,
Until the ear in Music's sweet abyss is hurled!

CXLVI.

The sailor o'er the blue sea sadly glides,
When first his native hills in mists are lost:
But fresh scenes in the ocean's azure tides,
Fresh isles when o'er that ocean he has crossed,
Those different scenes in which the soul gets tossed,
Oft make him disregard his friends behind.
But never—and may I not seem to boast—
Shall die, or grow faint in my attracted mind,
The affection for these Apennines—too strong its kind.

CXLVIII.

But let me enter Italy to muse:
Her rural theatre feels some relief
From lakes, trees, forests, dressed in summer's hues;
From fields o'er-bronzed with many a yellow sheaf.
Here choose a station: but the floods of grief
In this fast-fading clime must endless spring;
Recall her sons of talent! Let earth heave,
And burst her bosom's strength! then with new wing
Let the dead scorn their clay, and old days once more
bring.

CXLVIII.

Immortal recollections strew my path;
Ten thousand glorious footsteps here have been:
No curb was put on the Avenger's wrath;
Ah! her amazing lords no more are seen.
We feel their loss in this her sad serene.
No more with power darts the heroic eye,
Nor patriotic frenzy fires the spleen!
Even all her mighty men in ashes lie,
From Cicero, to her last child of majesty.

CXLIX.

When, like yon sun, Lucretius' talents rose,
No little of display her knowledge made;
As Græcia's matchless day began to close,
Her warrior masters slumbering in Death's shade.
The Muses left Greece' Helicon; Jove bade
Them in this favoured land their throne to rear,
Where they attained a most superior grade:
They made themselves renowned, and loved to wear
The plaited laurel for the sake of one so dear.

CL.

True; Alexander spread his conquests wide,
And made his Macedonia proudly tower;
He tore the haughty crest of India's pride,
And much curtailed base, upstart, nations' power:
But when did ever shine so bright an hour,
As that in which Augustus spread the fame
Of splendid literature; and gave a dower
To those who would for Science' summit aim;
And when they mounted there, smile on what they could claim?

CLI.

Can I express it?—no! I never can,
How that illustrious Cæsar merits praise;
Himself a paragon—a mighty man,
That made the seven hills with his lustre blaze!
The monarch of those immemorial days—
And what a monarch! Lives an emperor now,
On whom with such a rapture we might gaze;
Whose stately mien, eye, intellectual brow,
And answering actions, such a kingly champion show?

CLII.

Dear to the school-boy's heart is Virgil's lay;
The dreams he paints delight his passionate breast:
Away with modern poesy—away!
Allow him Virgil—this is his request.
He takes it into fields, and feels quite blest;
And 'mid wild mountains and wild valleys reads
His pastoral songs; while gazing towards the West,
Many a flock on emerald pasturage feeds,
And many a lowing herd recalls his matchless deeds.

CLIII.

Unalienable memory shall attach
The student's fondness, Virgil, e'er to thee;
In after days he ne'er shall find a match
To soothe his soul in hours of apathy:
And never shall he seem again to be
In contemplation 'mid his childhood's school,
Without being better able still to see
The guerdon of thy every golden rule;
And without owning thou art more than beautiful!

CLIV.

Lord of the thundering lyre! thou would'st have
broken
The strings of common harps, so frailly strung,
With which knight-errants ever gave the token
Of love, and 'neath the lady's window sung
In hours of gaudy moonlight. Yes! among
Heaven's citadels, all on thy lyre would doat,
In ears of startled gods it loudly rung;
Oh! could'st thou rise, again in music float
Beauteous Egeria's vales, and wake the ancient note!

CLV.

Fair Mantua! many a changing year has flown
Since Andes' village shed its last of smile;
Since Virgil, on the Mincius' banks alone,
Unbent his mind from literary toil.
Oh, Italy! it makes the wise recoil
To contemplate thy best scenes faded thus;
The change come o'er thy children and thy soil;
Now dying on the ear thy cities' buzz:
Yet this dark hour of death must be to all of us.

CLVI.

Thy happy valleys, Mantua, laugh no more;
They mourn even wreathed with Summer's glittering
"Happy!" an epithet for other shore; [corn:
The epithet for thee shall be "forlorn!"
Yet even in her ruins who can scorn
The land that such great geniuses once reared?
For here, the truly eminent were born;
E'en in Italia's past state, yet revered,
Lucretius, Virgil, Ovid,—godlike men appeared!

CLVII.

Know ye this pageant of peculiar kind,
When o'er an empire peeps the blinking morn;
And you behold its battlements, refined
By early twilight, gradually dawn?
Its pyramid-like towers, through tall mists borne,
Shine on your sight by beautiful degrees;
The proud flags floating, seeming heaven to scorn,
Its streets illumined grand as brazen seas;
Thus Science' empire glimmered on the World's dim ees.

CLVIII.

And when I viewed thee, matchless London, first,
In dalliance' majesty, in pompous shape;
Spanned by the sun's broad rays, thou didst outburst!
Cathedrals, towers, in one most gorgeous heap;
And thy two millions waking from their sleep!
At such an hour, upon thy "Monument,"
I stood and widely gazed; and thus did reap
The simile, that Science' kingdom rent
The august heavens as proudly, when to earth 'twas sent.

CLIX.

Yes! Ovid, how the poet's fire in thee
Sublimely flamed, yet in dread volumes shone,
When Ignorance' pile of huge-built vanity
Was by its burning glory melted down.
In vain it hurled far its demoniac frown!
For in those nations, clogged with darkness once,
Learning's strong sun burst through the clouds so dun,
And changed to lucid rainbows mists so dense;
Oh! Science, like the vulture, on her foe did pounce.

CLX.

I have stood on Chimborazo, and have seen
Heaven's elements show forth their majesty;
The thunderstorm's battalions intervene
'Tween its outrageous summits and the sky;
And marked the lightning fiercely flash, then die.
I too have heard this Asian mountain's rage
Roll back its peals of loud sublimity;
And, not cramped by five thousand years of age,
Beheld it cleave the monstrous clouds, as they engage!

CLXI.

And this is splendour! mortal, is it not;
When thy Almighty God, from Asia's tower,
Hurls upon quaking earth the blazing shot
That massive empires groan beneath the shower?
But in the mind of man, that puny bower,
Where Wisdom, quite unseen, in spirit sways
The sceptre of the world, gives to each hour
Its movements regular, the Almighty's rays
In more soul-striking splendour dwell, to pierce thy gaze!

CLXII.

Oft as a boy, in Learning's noblest halls,
Romantic thoughts kept flittering through my brain;
When autumn's sun did gild the school-room walls
Through the bright windows' every gleaming pane.
Schemes of ambition fired each youthful vein,
As I viewed its arched apertures of glass:
I mused on Frento's streams, and Horace' strain,
While images of ancient hours would pass
Of the "arva beata, divitesque insulas."

CLXIII.

O "happy fields, rich islands," no more glad!
Shall Horace ever sing again your praise?
Alas! unhonoured now ye seem, and sad,
Lost with the calendar of by-gone days.
O verses still divine, and classic lays!
O school-boy hours, O joyful times indeed!
Whene'er I see young striplings on their ways
To Science' turrets glittering o'er yon mead,
How have I thought on you, and felt my heart to bleed!

CLXIV.

Who reads the Alcaics and the Sapphics now,
Without his humble offering of thanks?
Many a triumphant student, round whose brow
The laurel has proclaimed to stand in ranks
Of Fame, is daily grateful. On the banks
Of Frento conjures he up Horace' sprite;
Earth is becoming haggard from the blanks
Of heroes half omnipotent. To-night
Their shades will meet you glistening with immortal might!

CLXV.

Ennobled Persius! thy discerning eye
Did nobly and consistently distress
Vice in her every form; not even shy
In piercing through an emperor's regal dress.
Nor would'st thou satirize these ages less;
For eighteen hundred years have piled a mass
For Folly that the dead would never guess,
Could they arise, and thus their judgments pass;
And every hour that rolls along, we sigh "Alas!"

CLXVI.

As purely did his fellow-satirist rise,
As strongly by his upraised brow revealing
Vice in her mildest airy shapes, as vice;
A heathen, yet endued with moral feeling!
And the Muse never, howe'er darkly stealing,
Found a polluted gross recess within
His most courageous genius. Virtue kneeling,
Acknowledged his efficiency to win,
From slavish paths of wrong, him deeming vice no sin.

CLXVII.

If judgment and experience we admire,
Let us a Juvenal adore: in him
Were these combined with intellectual fire.
Bright stars in yon vast area fairly swim;
Bright clouds of evening braid the horizon's rim—
Of more enduring character his aims:
He feared no emperor's threats, he spared no whim;
The clouds and stars shrink under Phœbus' flames,
His power outshone their rays, for nought such glory shames.

CLXVIII.

Adieu! Where now burns Vesta's ancient fire?
Where is the glorious old patrician race?
Where are the unvanquished heroes of the lyre?
Who fills their desolately-vacant place?—
Look at St. Peter's! there the sceptre, mace,
And eagle, thus degenerated lie;
While papal banners occupy that space
Where the Augustan standards used to fly;
Banners so dread defaced with Vice' vermilion dye!

CLXIX.

It makes the very blood to madly boil;
It makes the soul deliriously swell!
The haughty Vatican appears to smile,
Only exalted, when that empire fell—
When seeking gain from Heaven, it slaved for Hell!
On Rome's remains that palace-pile was built,
Piercing the loftiest clouds, its towers stand well;
But though those towers were gold, that palace gilt,
The Vatican must reel, and Vengeance' pit be filled!

CLXX.

There is an isle my boyhood loved—though I
Ne'er trode its radiant shores, its sands of pearl:
Good heavens! there meets you such an azure sky,
Ye never saw more blue-tinged waters curl—
The land that yields delight to rustic churl.
How beautiful it beams from open sea;
And sailors love the white sail to unfurl,
As they behold it, in the fire of glee,
Far glancing in the horizon of eternity.

CLXXI.

I read of it at school—its fields so fair,
Its mountains billowing with luxurious thyme;
The soothing pureness of its ocean air,
The freshness of its verdure so sublime.
And often have I in a vacant time
Thought of Ulysses on this pleasing isle;
And in my play-hours framed a little rhyme
Of all that hero's sufferings and toil,
On which most childish verse I now look on and smile.

CLXXII.

'Tis Sicily! In its green valleys sung
Philemon, Epicharmus, sons of Fame;
Theocritus, and others whom among
We feel the glorious thrill of Passion's flame.
The waves that wash its genial shore first came
From old Italia, its twin-sister dear:
They both shine through the sea just like some dream,
With ruined monuments, still glittering clear,
Fast by their sea-shore on huge rocks that yield one fear.

CLXXIII.

Hail, climes around! where many a pilgrim smiles,
(High perched on some gigantic sea-girt brow,)
On gleaming beautifully-sprinkled isles,
Round whose fair coasts cerulean waters flow.
Sicilia sees her offspring near her grow,
Who, like sweet Thetis, joys within her soul.
Oh, as in far, far distance bright they glow,
And on the pilgrim's eyes their glories roll,
He deems them islands of the blest in skylight's goal.

CLXXIV.

Hail, lands, which in the Italian night full beam,
Like starry beauty-spots on ocean's face,
Shedding to heaven your most delicious gleam,
Each streak as fine as some gold needle's trace.
Oh, Aphrodite sanctifies your space!
Cities of Paradise, in costly sheen,
Seem all embroidered with thin moonlight lace;
And houris walk along their streets serene,
With robes of beauty ever white and purely clean.

CLXXV.

Smile, ye Æolian breezes! ever fan
These pleasant regions of your native site;
Cool all their blossoms that are dim and wan,
Let a propitious climate heal with might.
Smile, ye Æolian breezes! still smile bright,
And make their ocean ripple with glad wave,
Form paths for Hesperus in the tinselled night:
And, O kind Heaven, let some young star-beam pave
These paths with gold, to keep it from a watery grave.

CLXXVI.

But Meditation, tripping on quite gay
From isle to adjoining isle, from sphere to sphere,
Ah! as she speeds so laughing in her way,
Is struck quite suddenly with wild despair.
Reader, I must now write as if even there,
Therefore o'er-look the language of the Muse;
Alas! scenes tarnished that were once so fair,
So chequered with the most delightful hues;
How soon the streaks of loveliness their radiance lose!

CLXXVII.

Musing in Sicily's still famous isle,*
Indulging in a wide north-eastward glance,
I light on Ætna, a tremendous pile,
Which occupies the empyrean's broad expanse.
The forge of Vulcan, who supplied the wants
Of the Almighty Thunderer, and wrought
Plenipotent huge bolts; this mountain plants
In giddy clouds its vertex passing thought; [sought.
Whose crater has heaven's arch of fabled brass long

* As I was in the midst of this poem, the news came over to England of the fearful explosion of Ætna; which caused me to attempt its description.

CLXXVIII.

It swaggers most enormous, flouts the sky,
Scowls on the ocean, numbers all the ships;
And many a seaman does it terrify,
When it wraps sky and earth in black eclipse.
For you must know some horrid Fury rips
At times its bulk, of greatness beating word;
And in the burning flames her snake-hair dips,
Then wrings her hissing locks, till earth gets surd
With stunning peals, cries, shrieks, such as ye never heard.

CLXXIX.

Imagination strengthen me to arm
The gulph of Thought in terrible array!
I sing not now of woman's blissful charm,
Of her dark eye, her fairy step so gay;
Or merely of proud Battle's pompous day;
Or of entrancing scenes which thrill the heart:
But sing the fire of Ætna! which shall weigh
On many a feeling one like sorrow's dart,
And make the reader shudder oft, and wildly start!

CLXXX.

Morn's light broke forth, of woe no warning given;
The white-washed hamlets round old Ætna gleamed;
A little smoke wound its smooth way to heaven;
So silvery shone, ye might have thought ye dreamed.
The fields so fertile, like the emerald, beamed:
The azure sky looked placid on the earth;
Along its blue the laughing sun-rays streamed;
The green leaves of the forest danced in mirth;
Each opening flower seem'd striving to display its worth.

CLXXXI.

The day went on—the husbandman to work
As usual went, and first his children bless'd;
And nothing could his grateful spirit irk,
He kissed his wife, and felt his soul at rest.
After he had his family caressed,
His spade and rake, and other tools, he took,
Then plodded to the fields in verdure dressed:
And oft he would above benignant look;
As he felt need of Him who ne'er the good forsook.

CLXXXII.

Small children of the villages were playing,
Some this, some that, and some another game:
The rustic half-grown lad was idly straying,
Whose love of honesty was all his fame.
He watched the sea-birds as they near him came,
And wished that, like them, he had pinions too;
Then would he visit Phœbus' gorgeous flame,
And not tread earth, but skim yon smiling blue;
And many other mighty wonders he would do.

CLXXXIII.

God's way is in the whirlwind! who can tell
Even what a fleeting hour may soon bring forth?
The sea once smooth He makes a boiling hell,
And turns the calm to furiousness of wrath!
The blue sky He can in one moment scathe;
The word He speaks, the Nile is clotted blood!
Oh, how mysterious is the Almighty's path!
The Archangel has before Him trembling stood,
And how shall man endure the torrents of His flood?

CLXXXIV.

But turn to Ætna. What escapes its verge?
Long wreaths of smoke are curling from its top:
First a weak flame its progress seems to urge—
The dwellers in its vales are looking up.
The empyrean boils with red, and seems to droop
As in a moment with sulphureous clouds,
Which round its shattered crest begin to grope,
Enlarging on one like the Judgement's shrouds,
Or like contorted Hydras twisting—hateful crowds!

CLXXXV.

And worse, far worse, the prospect is becoming:
The wavy hills around, which looked so green,
The leaden weight of smoke is now benumbing,
And an unsightly fog doth intervene.
No more can I survey the ocean scene,
The hamlets seem to melt in awe away:
Disturbance clatters! and the sunlight sheen
Cannot expand its vivifying ray;
For black clouds gallop o'er it in the realms of day.

CLXXXVI.

I stand upon the Apennines afar;
Pliny's ambition never shall be mine:
I stand to contemplate this heavy war
'Tween earth, heaven, ocean. In enormous line
The mountains with a gradual flickering shine;
The sea-birds to their crag-hewn lodgings fly—
They shriek most fearful, by instinct divine;
And from the rocky clefts their young ones cry,
As they behold such horrors darkling in the sky.

CLXXXVII.

Fate! hold on high thy arm of sovereignty,
And pencil on that scowl what one may read;
Give me the bright torch of Philosophy,
That I may understand, why this dread deed.
Alas! it cannot exposition need;
'Tis the small miniature of that last day,
When the vast globe shall to like woes succeed,
And in one ball of terrible array,
Like to a shortly-blazing meteor pass away!

CLXXXVIII.

Mid-day has passed—with it, its azure beams:
An isle of fire in billows of the air,
Girt by rough oceans, hued with crimson gleams,
The sun darts forth! and woods and mountains stare.
And one imagines, gazing upward there,
In the red-hot abyss Charybdis boils;
While great clouds tumble through it in despair,
Assuming forms of tottering castled piles;
Beneath them sinks the firmament—my heart recoils!

CLXXXIX.

Lo! on the huge horizon you can trace
A figure robed in horrible array;
Clotted with blood and smoke, is Nature's face,
That nymph so beautiful in month of May;
Who then has her waist girt with daisies gay,
With harebells, thyme, which dangle in the breeze.
Her veins appear to broadly swell, and weigh
O'er her distorted forehead. All her trees
Flash forth, like towers of brass, o'er-beetling gory seas.

CXC.

The vault of heaven is burst with spreading flames;
The lightning's falchion cleaves the clouds so black;
And grim-eyed Vengeance his dire javelin aims
At Earth. Ah! sweet Hope writhes on Ruin's rack—
Desist, ye elements! alack, alack!
Are your ears deaf to those wild frenzied yells?
A lovely female's prayers entreat you back,
Whose shrill, heart-rending shriek like thunder swells!
I see the maniac listening to some demon's spells.

CXCI.

Strange sight! Oh, surely Fate unfurls its wings,
For she, not suffocated, sweeps through flames;
Then standing o'er the blazing gulph, now wrings
Her hands on high; and joy unnatural teems
Within her rolling eyes, as if the dreams
Of heaven descended through ambrosial showers.
Alas! she e'en mistakes these glaring streams,
And deems them golden springs, 'stead of hell's powers;
Thus thinking, leaps she down the abyss!—Speed on ye hours!

CXCII.

Fancy the scene: the rustic no more dreaming,
But rushing in mad frenzy to his home;
The little children now in horror screaming,
Trying within their mother's breast the doom
Of terror to avert. Within a room
Of his most humble cottage wildly plays
The husbandman, who hears the far loud boom
Of fierce Gibello bursting in dread ways;
'Tis suicide to rush out, and here he shuddering stays!

CXCIII.

But as he offers up his prayers to God,
His children rend the very roof with cries;
While ever and anon, with aspect rude,
The wild and frantic mother views the skies;
With hair all loose, with madly upraised eyes,
She bursts the cottage door;—and hears dread noise,
Down heaven's seared battlements, while rudely rise
Clouds red as blood which whistling whirlwinds poise;
She shrieks, then falls down dead! Farewell to earthly joys!

CXCIV.

Farewell! What comes? Outrageous brimstone rolls,
Tumbling in crimson billows through the heaven!
Not Sodom languished under fiercer coals
Than those along the aerial precincts driven.
The sky scowls like the "Giant's Causeway" given
To furious conflagrations, fearful gleams;
Stones whizz afar, and lava seems to have striven
The blue air to contaminate with streams
Of most polluting colour, tinged with hideous beams.

CXCV.

Good heavens! the very mountain torn in two,
And stripped by Vengeance of its shaggy hide,
Distends, like Hell's red furnace, to the view!
Oh, could ye see it as it opens wide!
An earthly purgatory to abide
Within five miles of the dishevelled mass!
Oh! could ye mark the grinning demons glide,
And hear their wild song as they wildly pass
Down, down the slippery brimstone, ranged in Battle's class:

THE DEMONS' SONG.

"It opens fiery, fiery! and it glares!
Each giant eye of it so glassy stares;
Its head is red with blood-bedabbled hairs!

"But we can here carouse as if in hell,
As when our eyes on Stygian frenzy dwell!
Oh, yes! oh, yes! we love these horrors well!

"Shoot! shoot! noise after noise, and rumbling roll!
The village bells are moaning, toll, toll, toll!
But the sound falls most sweet on Demons' soul!

"We sit in huge fires, and devour the flames;
No vengeance e'er the Demon's nature tames,
For the most horrid thing no Demon shames!

"But its huge trunk, whose measure none can learn,
See how it does the flaming volumes spurn!
For it will one day all creation burn!

"Let us away now—far away, away!
The fire is now faint, and Time's eve is grey;
For a hundred new spirits howl in hell to-day!"

CXCVI.

What is that horribly appalling form?
Is it Typhæus bursting through his tomb,
Piling big battlements above this storm,
To trouble Heaven once more to fix his doom?—
Vulcan runs frantic from his fiery room,
And seeing the monster towering up so vain,
He swiftly fells him with a blazing boom;
Who from his hundred mouths roars out with pain;
Then sinks beneath red Sicily in chains again!

CXCVII.

Now waxes faint the fire on Ætna's height;
No flaming surge now dashes thro' the sky,
The blood-stained clouds no longer sweep with might,
The sun no longer starts, as if 'twould die!—
But tinges on the horizon one can spy,
And gradually ocean's sweet blue opes:
Added to this, the moon's unsullied eye
Beams, like a lovely woman's, as it droops
So languishingly beautiful, so fair with hopes.

CXCVIII.

'Tis grand, in mid-sea where the blue waves roar,
To view the Atlantic and Pacific rolled
Together, sweeping from each distant shore,
And blazing near each other, like rich gold!
'Tis grand to see the Equator wide unfold
Its mountain shoulders to uplift stout ships;
And with its mighty measuring line so old
Divide the pompous globe; then with its lips
Kiss Cancer and famed Capricorn tinged with gay stripes.

CXCIX.

But here what ugly splendour,—we may term
It frightful, wild magnificence, to mark
Ætna burst open, parching many a germ,
And threatening Sicily with each red spark;
Hurling most burning stones, and heaven their mark;
Deluging villages with floods of fire;
More noisy than fierce Cerberus' thunder-bark
At Hell's vile portals; belching with such ire
Hot brimstone, as to make the seamen near expire!

CC.

The flame is o'er, it will not harm again;
The fire is over—but the deed is done;
The fire is over—but its spoils remain.
Ah! many a lovely eye, which thousands won,
Shall no more gaze upon the morning sun
Flushing the glittering surface of the sea,
Waking Sicilia's hills: no more shall run,
In gladsome sport, the happy boys to see
Some arbour dear, where rainbow showers they used to flee.

CCI.

Their last home is not in the ocean fields,
Where countless heroes in their glory lie:
Their last home 's not 'neath churchyard elm which yields
A sacred spell to draw relations nigh;
Where friends plant flowers on graves of friends that die;
And every sunny Sabbath seems to smile
On little children strewing beauteously
A few geraniums, thus to bloom awhile
On their dear mother's grave, their memory to beguile.

CCII.

No, no! the mother and the child fare like;
The horrid foam of madness their lips steeps;
The dead babes in the dust a terror strike
Into the soul! Even Death for his ire weeps!
'Mid suffocating fumes, and burning deeps,
'Mid ashes, bitumen, and fiery coals,
The chill of icy fate upon them creeps,
The savage wrath of Ætna o'er them rolls;
And anywhere they lie—a heap of mangled souls!

CCIII.

Now daylight's beams more beautifully glow,
And gleam full brightly to the distant gaze,
As they expand on the horizon's brow,
Meeting the purple water with their rays.
They streak the round sea like most radiant lace,
That ocean seems to laugh among her isles;
Nature now flashes with a delicate grace,
And Amphitrite puts on her heavenliest smiles;
Neptune waves his huge trident ravished with her wiles.

CCIV.

Oh! what a calmness reigns—a calm so strange!
An exquisite, sweet calm! The noisy claps
Of Ætna are now fled. Tremendous change! [raps
Peace flower-wreathed, with her gentle handmaid,
At Ruin's door; it opes—she sees the shapes
Of many of her loved children turned to dust:
Despair, now million-mouthed, within the gaps
Of his unmeasured jaws dares even to thrust
The helpless babes so chill, so cold. Yet Heaven is just.

CCV.

She starts! then recollects herself—and prays.
Her blue eyes glimmer on yon future world;
I cannot well interpret what she says;
But her fine lip, in triumph's grandeur curled,
Insinuates, that though her sons are hurled
To death so violent, yet their enemies
Shall in a fathomless abyss be whirled
By Justice' angry billows; nor shall rise
Ever again from this dark den of miseries.

CCVI.

How lovely looks she on Sicilia's isle!
Just now the swarthy figure of Despair,
Without a ray of light, without a smile,
His brow enlarging, like a night of care,
I saw, instead of Peace, and Mercy fair,
Her handmaid. Oh, 'tis very beautiful!
I wish the thoughtless world could this sight share;
And then its iron heart would not be dull
In uttering an expression of the Almighty's rule!

CCVII.

But while considering Ætna's broken mass,
Full flames to me the furnace of the heart,
A furnace of a more prodigious class; [smart
Which burns in Time, which burns in hell, whose
Shall by no power be quenched, nor e'er depart,
Though million thunderstorms should rain united,
And let their monstrous drops upon it dart!
Oh, terrible impressions too long slighted!
Oh, fire of wrath, where Justice ne'er can be requited!

CCVIII.

A fierce sigh billows in my breast—Ah, me!
Feeling's door opes, the cankering serpent bites.
Yes; as I trace yon blue Eternity
Studded with beautifully-glittering lights,
The contrast my mind gives of wars and fights,
Of Passion's battles, makes my brain to reel:
Conviction, Ætna's horrors, each thing blights
The soothing peace I otherwise might feel;
Would that were beaten soft as flesh this heart of
steel.

CCIX.

There are, we all well know, these sober hours;
When Contemplation, frenzied at our deeds,
Makes them scowl, like demoniacal powers,
Until the stony soul with horror bleeds!
The garden of the heart o'er-run with weeds;
Where blooming flowers ought long since to have
And shed their perfume o'er the mental meads, [grown,
Enjoying Conscience' sunlight from her throne;
But instead killing this poor frame with many a groan.

CCX.

I've loved to see in church the little child,
Kneel by its mother's side, and look towards heaven;
So pure, so innocent, so meekly mild,
Seeming to wish that nothing should be given
To it but God's own blessing: it has striven,
And clasped its gentle hands more tightly still,
As if it feared its Maker should be driven
Away, by doing its devotions ill:
No sight could ever more my inmost bosom thrill!

CCXI.

Oh! shall I plunge myself in Ætna's flame!
When I remember that I once thus knelt
Beside my parents, lisping out the name,
The grand name of Jehovah!—then I felt!
My boyish heart, I recollect, would melt,
As some fine Scripture-piece each young nerve struck.
Farewell, ye halcyon days! so shortly dealt:
No more by righteous pastures, and clear brook,
I now glad wander! Stop, and see Gibello's look

CCXII.

Yet 'tis not that my innumerable faults
May be, or may not be, of foulest dye:
There is a boundless Justice which ne'er halts
Between two vain opinions' mystery;
That Justice will condemn the Pharisee:
The niceness of the action palliates not;
The exterior mien may never testify,
Nor man's vain eyes observe sin's lurking spot,—
Yet he may have that which shall cause his soul to rot.

CCXIII.

Transcendent thought! that man is not our judge.
On mountain parapets I mock, I scorn,
Man's paltry ways and works; yet bear no grudge.
Not mine to seek revenge, tho' I were torn
In sunder by abuses—of all shorn.
Behold distorted Ætna—such is hate,
A frightful monster, ragged and forlorn;
Too mild a simile. Unbar yon gate
Of Hell, and fiends will portrait it in truest state!

CCXIV.

Abominable choice! How could I ever
Relinquish Nature's amiable mountains,
The blue sea, the blue sky, the placid river,
The vernal vales, the lily-bordered fountains,
For the world's rampant riot? How it pains
Me now to think I could its friendship claim!
Alas! my mind is black with dreadful stains,
My cheek now mantles with the blush of shame,
And God alone can the apostate sinner tame.

CCXV.

I stand in nakedness—all disarrayed!
The castles that I built are tumbled down,
Their battlements of splendour melt and fade,
All, like the insubstantial dream, have flown.
Stop—listen! did I not just hear the groan
Of many a virtuous thought which armed the walls
Of the Soul's palace?—hark! a dying moan!
A horrid shriek upon my ear now falls—
Religion, dabbled in Crime's gore, my sight appals!

CCXVI.

Nor would I put a razor to my throat,
Or tie the murderous cord around my neck;
Tho' many with such dark ideas have fought,
They have done this. And tho' I am a wreck
Of what I was; yet Heaven has pleased to check
Ideas that so abominable are.
Thus armoured, I shall not yield to the beck
And call of Hell's Archangel everywhere,
When his soft whisper rolls like thunder thro' my ear.

CCXVII.

But we are all apostates. Once there stood
Around the sacred font our sponsors dear;
They made a vow in the most serious mood
That Nature can for us; there did appear
Upon their brows a staid religious fear.
The water bathed our infant forehead o'er,
And the most Holy Dove descended there,
And lit the childish heart, which seemed to soar
To heaven with that pure Dove, till it was seen no more.

CCXVIII.

But who has held inviolate that vow,
Confirmed in after years? who dare to meet
God in the whirlwind, or on Sinai's brow?
None! none! But give me pinions to my feet!
On Zion, near to Salem, smiles He sweet:
I will go there, this very moment go,
And with a rended heart will I entreat
That He would purify me, white as snow,
That He would cause me each most trivial sin to know.

CCXIX.

Enough upon this head. I may have tired
The world with mountain-visions; yet I wot
That when the bosom's depths are thorned and briared,
Choked up with weeds, we must indulge the thought:
The thoughts so wild, so mad, we long have sought,
Yet would not seek, to know; but onward spurred
To the pursuit, in dread collision brought
Virtue and Vice, they speaking, to be heard
Within the mental vestibule, each angry word.

CCXX.

On divers fairy things could I expand,
On mermen, on mermaids; on fairy tales
Made in the "Arabian Nights" to appear so grand;
On Tigris' streams, on Bagdat's gilted walls;
And many a dream that childhood's bliss recalls:
But Time permits me not to dwell on these;
And Memory, musing on that dear time, wails
Because those raptures manhood fail to please,
Borne on dark-floating tides to Lethe's awful seas.

CCXXI.

Innocent joys of boyhood, how ye passed!
How soon your healthiest sun of glory set!
And manhood's strength a fleeting time will last,
Then hoary age the mastery will get.
The silvery hair, as snow-white as the sleet,
Shall take the place of that once raven-black;
The staff shall soon befriend the tottering feet;
The once strong frame shall writhe upon the rack
Of grim Disease, to make us wish our childhood back!

CCXXII.

O thou false world! the parent of deceit!
Thy promises are odious; and thy smiles
Are adder-stings; thy forms of truth a cheat!
Thy mightiest efforts fraught with selfish wiles.
The spirit Nature gave me e'er reviles
Thy promises, smiles, truth, and friendship—all!
For thy best joy some empty hour beguiles,
Which, had we not had, we would ne'er recall:
No! never can I at thy hateful footstool fall!

CCXXIII.

If the world read these lines, they deem it well;
If the world read them not, yet still the same.
Away with its vile flattery! as the spell
Of flattery I ever deemed a name.
Ambition's laurels, honour, grandeur, fame,
If the world's gift, must soon dissolve and fade;
Too oft such glory only ends in shame;
And thousands wish, who reach its loftiest grade,
On their death-bed that they had lived in humbler shade.

CCXXIV.

All that I ask for is a mother's smile,
A father's blessing, heaven's most precious store!
I crave a brother's tear to pay my toil,
When he shall read my book in noontide's hour;
And think he sees 'mid fancy's dreamy shower,
That one who left his isle in boyhood's day;
And that my sisters, in their garden bower,
May muse on him o'er ocean far away,
And spend one idle hour upon his *simple* lay.

THE END.

PRINTED BY METCALF AND PALMER, CAMBRIDGE.

Printed in Dunstable, United Kingdom

91218895R00097